The Christian's Guide To Effective Personal Management

Other works by Kenneth W. Oosting, Ph.D.:

Book:

> *Strategic Planning for Private Higher Education* (Binghamton, NY: The Haworth Press, 1997), with Carle M. Hunt, Robert E. Stevens, David Loudon, and R. Henry Migliore.

Modular courses developed for Degree Completion Programs and being offered at colleges and universities in the U.S. and Canada:

> Business Information and Decision Making
> Case Studies in Ethics
> Case Studies in Leadership
> Case Studies in Leadership and Management
> Christian Ethics
> Christian World View
> Communication Concepts
> Cutting Issues in Management
> Goals, Priorities and Attitudes
> Making of the Modern Mind
> Management Principles
> Managing People: Groups and Leadership
> Managing People in Organizations
> Managing Work and Organizations
> Special Topics in U.S. History

The Christian's Guide To Effective Personal Management

by

Kenneth W. Oosting, Ph.D.

Franklin, Tennessee

Paperback edition
ISBN 0-9645014-6-5

First edition, 1997
First printing

Printed in the United States of America

Editor: Sharon Landers, Ph.D.
Quality Control: Kathy Zeigler, B.S.M.
Cover Design: Jennifer O. Shaw, Ricardo E. Rios

Unless otherwise indicated, all Scripture quotations are taken from the *Holy Bible, New International Version*, copyright © 1973, 1978, 1984 by the International Bible Society.

For information and orders please contact:

JKO Publishing
200 Seaboard Lane
Franklin, TN 37067
615/771-7705
fax: 615/771-7810
e-mail: books@jkop.com

Dedication

This book is dedicated to my wife, Jackie Oosting, for her help, for being patient and for encouraging me toward the completion of this book. She has provided many of the concepts used in the book and over the past two years has endured many hours while I was cloistered in the study working on the research or writing. Thanks, Jackie.

Many of my observations on life which are reflected in this book come from my parents, Adrian J. and Marguerite F. Oosting. They are now at their ninety-sixth and ninety-fourth birthdays, respectively, and have been married for seventy-two years. They live in North Muskegon, Michigan.

Thanks to the many people who have worked with me, encouraged and otherwise helped to provide the thoughts contained in this book. A special thanks goes to our four children, their spouses and our six grandchildren for my perspectives on life that they have helped to form. We are proud of them all. The grandchildren, John Robert, Amanda, Hannah, Alex, Drew and Rachel, are a source of great joy to us.

This book would not have come about without the expert care at JKO Publishing of Dr. Sharon Landers (who edited the book), Kathy Zeigler (who did the proofreading), Jackie Oosting (who worked with the printing company) and Jennifer Shaw (who prepared the cover).

Several people who have gone on to be with the Lord have served as role models for me. They include Ken Barnhard (Muskegon, Michigan), Howard Altman (Dade City, Florida), Doris LeBron (Gainesville, Florida), Dr. Donald Luck (New Cumberland, Pennsylvania) and Ken DeLora (Muskegon, Michigan).

Thanks to many others for the illustrations, ideas, Christian role models, inspiration and other help in writing this book. God has been present in how we are able to help one another to do the work of the Kingdom.

TABLE OF CONTENTS

Preface

Life presents constant challenges. Some of these challenges are opportunities, some are problems. Although we can rely upon others to help us meet these challenges, other people have their own challenges to face. In fact, others will come to us for help with their challenges. Human beings have a limited capacity to meet their challenges. How can we use this capacity to meet the challenges and survive to live again another day?

The Christian adds God to the arsenal for meeting these challenges. Through Bible study and prayer, the Christian can withstand any challenge. We are not told it would be easy. But we can do it.

But how do we do it? How should we go about managing the process of survival? Do we gird ourselves to meet each challenge through an effective defense? While defense is important, this book suggests that each Christian should develop a proactive plan for setting goals, setting priorities and determining strategies.

It is my hope that this book will stir you to become involved in being responsible for your own life through proactive planning. Only you can effectively implement and utilize the talents God has provided for you. One segment of this book is devoted to helping you explore the spiritual aspect of the self.

Let me know about success stories you and others have experienced in setting goals, priorities and strategies while meeting the challenges of life.

Kenneth W. Oosting
Franklin, Tennessee

Chapter One

Managing Yourself: The Prerequisites

The person who observes that the world could be better than it is and decides to do something about it, must first start with an examination of and then action related to self in order to be equipped to bring about that change. — Kenneth W. Oosting

I choose to be happy today. — Norma Zimmer

Why Manage Yourself?

These pages are not written for the fainthearted. They are intended for those who have come to the conclusion that life itself could be better and that they are the chief architects of making life better. This chapter begins with the conclusion that managing yourself has certain prerequisites, things you must address effectively in order to achieve effective personal management. Only persons who are willing to address these prerequisites can be helped by this book. Others will have to accept what life dishes out as a result of being unwilling to assume a degree of responsibility for the future.

Unless we die now, each of us will have a future. Some of us will control important parts of our futures. Some of us will let others control our futures. Which one you will be is up to you, regardless of who you are today. No excuses. You are the person you have chosen to be, and you will become the person you choose to become. Unless you live in slavery, you are in charge of your life. Whether it is an enjoyable life, a life that contributes to making life better for others, is up to you — not your parents (unless you are still a child), not your spouse or a friend, not the government and not society. It's up to you. Sobering thought?

When Should You Manage Yourself?

If you still think taking charge of your life might be worthwhile, read on. You have two choices — to accept life as it is or be willing to do something about it. If you want to bring about some changes, the following are some of the hurdles you must consider. I urge you to consider each of the prerequisites (required first steps) and apply them to your personal situation. Then you can ask yourself, "Am I willing to address these issues thoroughly and carefully and then act if I do not already meet the prerequisites?"

But before we talk about the prerequisites, let's look at the assumptions that I have made in developing the prerequisites. These assumptions underlie everything you will read in this book. I assume these to be true. If you do not, then you might not want to accept this approach. My guess, however, is that most of you will concur with these assumptions. It will be helpful to discuss them here so that you will be mindful of them as you read further in the book.

What Does It Mean To Manage Yourself?

Some of the underlying assumptions in this book relating to effective personal management are:

• Each of us must recognize that God created us with the ability and the opportunity to make choices. It is up to us to make wise choices in a manner that will bring honor and glory to Him. We make wise choices when we take charge of our own lives, remain focused upon clear goals and choose to manage our lives effectively.

• All of us, if of reasonably sound mind and body, are capable of effectively managing ourselves. This comes from the abilities we are born with, our God-given talents and gifts, plus our education and experience. Our development and preparation is also based upon the influence that other people and events have had upon us as we mature.

• There is much we can learn from others that we can apply in our efforts to manage ourselves effectively. We learn both positive and negative things from others; we learn what to strive toward and what we wish to avoid. All of us constantly learn from other people around us.

• God wants us to manage ourselves effectively as part of the scriptural admonitions He gave to us about the development of our Christian faith and its application in the world in which we live.

• Each of us seeks happiness, and we do it in terms that are meaningful to us individually. We will be happier if we are able to understand what is personally meaningful and the means of effectively attaining that meaningfulness which comes from effectively managing ourselves.

- When we ourselves are effectively managed, we are then in a position to help others manage themselves effectively; we can help others rather than be in a position of demanding help from others (read *contribute to* rather than *take from* society).

- To be effective Christians, we must first be effective human beings. We cannot know God very well if we carry with us a bag of personal problems that demands much or all of our time and thus prevents us from having a relationship with God that directs our lives.

- All of us are "more together" at some times than at other times. During periods of stress, all of us should be free to draw upon the strength of others. The amount of stress we experience that has no major causative factor is a direct indicator of whether we are effectively managing ourselves.

- Each of us has a different set of spiritual gifts or talents. Each of us has at least one and some have many spiritual gifts. Our personal management requires us to discover these gifts, to accept what they are, to sharpen them through education and experience and then to use the gifts in ways that are consistent with our faith and other values.

- A regular, sustained relationship with God is essential for the effective personal management of the Christian. Without it we lack focus and a clear reason for our existence. A dynamic relationship with God is possible only through regular prayer, Bible study and dedicated quiet time with God.

- We all need focus in our lives. When we drift from day to day without a clear set of purposes or guides, we live our lives on the basis of the pressures others place upon us, Christians and non-Christians alike. Without focus in our lives, we only know our histories (and our histories only if we pause to look at what we have been doing). With focus in our lives, we concentrate on what we wish to be and thus eliminate the things which do not contribute to what is in our focus.

- To have focus in life, we must have faith in God that we understand and that is not filled with doubt (although most of us have a reasonable level of doubt). Then we must develop purposes that relate to what we wish to accomplish while on this earth. We must understand our priorities within those purposes or goals. We must work out strategies to accomplish these goals or purposes. Each strategy must include the education and experience that the focus requires. Then we must have the resolve to carry out what is within our focus with the help of God and others.

- Effectively managed persons will seek to make the world they know better as a result of their lives as measured in the lives of contemporaries and those who will live in the world thereafter. This does not require us to be a Thomas Edison or make contributions on the scale that he did. It does require that, in some ways, the world is a happier place in which to live as a result of our having been in it and that our lives are enriching or have enriched the faith of others. We will not always know the positive effects we have had on others, but we can be sure that we have affected thousands of others during our lifetimes.

- The measure of effectively managed persons will be demonstrated more by the impact they have on the people who are around them each day than by those who see them at less frequent intervals. We cannot save our impact for those occasions when we are more public because those around us each day know the kind of persons we really are. These people are affected by us and we by them.

- If we do not effectively manage ourselves, after childhood no one will be able to do it for us. Regardless of how little we decide to allow others to control our lives, effective personal management cannot happen until we assume responsibility for our own lives. For example, while Paul talks of wives submitting themselves to their husbands,[1] he also talks to women about assuming responsibility for their own behavior (taking charge of their own personal management).[2] For men, Paul tells us that to effectively manage ourselves, we must first be willing to love others, a feat difficult for many men.[3]

• As the children of parents, we were all born into families, and all of us are destined to go through life in the company of others. An effectively managed person will have a positive relationship with others and, through that relationship, have a positive effect upon them as well as learn from them. If we cannot learn easily from others, we have yet to develop effective, positive relationships with them.

What Are The Prerequisites?

And now, let's look at the twelve prerequisites for effective personal management that each of us must consider.

1. Being Right With God

All a man's ways seem right to him, but the Lord weighs the heart. —Proverbs 21:2

Pride goes before destruction, a haughty spirit before a fall.— Proverbs 16:18

That everyone who believes in him may have eternal life. For God so loved the world, that he gave his one and only Son, that whoever believes in him shall not perish but have eternal life. For God did not send his Son into the world to condemn the world, but to save the world through him. Whoever believes in him is not condemned, but whoever does not believe stands condemned already, because he has not believed in the name of God's one and only Son. This is the verdict: Light has come into the world, but men loved darkness instead of light because their deeds were evil. Everyone who does evil hates the light, and will not come into the light, for fear that his deeds will be exposed. But whoever lives by the truth comes into the light, so that it may be seen plainly that what he has done has been done through God. — John 3:15-21

Too much attention to self is probably the major reason that people are not at peace with God. Slothfulness, or laziness, is probably second. Most of us are involved with both in varying degrees. Attention to self becomes a stumbling block only when it is out of proportion. Slothfulness, on the other hand, is never a desirable attribute. Why is attention to self only a problem when it reaches high proportions? It is because each of us must have a healthy level of self-respect in order to function in this world. As will be discussed later, a healthy self-respect is a matter of balance. The mature person we will describe later has achieved this balance.

Having a right relationship with God requires us to put God first in a meaningful way and not just by the words that we say. Having God first means giving God the firstfruits of our time, our talent, our money and our attention. How many of us are really ready to do this? The implication of putting God first is that we must put self in at least second place (after God). To what extent is that a problem for you?

Chapter Three will further explore the idea of being right with God. There are no absolute standards by which we can tell if the relationship is right or not. However, we tend to know when it is right based upon how we feel about the situation. When we are confused, are not certain about ourselves or about God and are determined to do what will bring pleasure to ourselves, we can be quite sure that our relationships with God need help, that we need to come closer to God and that this closeness must be a result of our actions rather than waiting for God. God is ready for us all the time. He waits on us. We must take the action to close the gap.

When we are in a right relationship with God, we are probably in a good relationship with ourselves. We recognize that we are important and that we have value in this world, but we recognize that God is first.

What does it require to meet this prerequisite? It requires that we assume the responsibility for having our relationships with God be as they should be. As mentioned above, God is ready for us. He is unchanging. He waits for us. We must take the step to bring ourselves closer to God.

A sign in front of a church I once saw said, "If you're not as close to God as you once were, who moved?" The obvious answer is, "not God." We move closer to and then away from God throughout our lives. Even those who remain quite close to God will have times when they move a small (or possibly a great) distance from God. It is a constant struggle to constrain our selfish natures in order to move toward a closer relationship with God.

How can we make the move that will bring us closer to God? There are several steps involved:

- We must cultivate our thinking processes in order to communicate with and think about God constantly. Not easy to do but it can become a habit.[4]

- We must pray frequently. Once-a-day prayer is not adequate. Prayers can be long or short. They can be on a single topic or include everything that is on our hearts.[5]

- We must read the Bible. As we come to a deeper understanding of God's Word, we come more fully to understand God and His relationship with us.[6]

- We must have fellowship with other Christians. In this way we help other Christians, and we allow them to help us in remaining steadfast in our Christian lives. The other side of this is to avoid the company of persons who, directly or indirectly, lead us to enter into thoughts and actions that are contrary to our Christian faith. This includes both people and influences such as the books and magazines we read, the places we go, what we watch on television and the thoughts that we engage in during the day.[7]

2. Being Right With The World

Just as we must be right with God, we must find a right relationship with all the persons we interact with in the world. While this will mostly be people, we also have to be reconciled with where we live, our education, our economic situation, our work, our church, our geographical location and many more related physical things. Have you ever heard people grumble about their situations in life, such as where they live, yet they are not willing or do not have an understanding of what it takes to make a change in a specific situation? Sometimes people enjoy grumbling. Sometimes we grumble about things around us when our unhappiness is actually within ourselves. We must come to peace with what we cannot or will not change and determine to change that part of our lives that makes us unhappy.

Then, there are people. Most of us get along with some people better than others. A few people seem to get along with everyone. We might admire those people, but we assume that they will always be different from us. Some people frustrate us. Others anger us. Some we just don't like. Yet God commands us to love one another.

That gives concern to many of us. We tend to think that certainly God didn't mean to include this person or that person. They are so obnoxious that not even God could love them. Yet we know that is not what the Bible says. The prerequisite is that we must be at peace with others in the world. This might mean that we must take action to repair or build a relationship with someone where an unfortunate break has taken place.

There is also the penalty, the cost, we incur when we strongly dislike someone. That internal anger or frustration tends to be destructive to us. It brings out a negative side in us. It tends to bother us, makes us feel uneasy. How can we make it right?

Some years ago I received a letter from a young woman who had been my student when I was a college professor. She had gone on to a Bible college and someone there had apparently confronted her about having right relationships with everyone in the world. As a result, she wrote me a letter in which she apologized for having cheated on a test in a course I taught. She regretted having done this and asked that her confession would restore her right relationship with me. Notice that it had not been a problem for me. I did not know she had cheated on the test. I was proud that one of my former students had gone on to a Bible college to prepare herself for some form of Christian service. The letter and my return letter of assurance restored our relationship as far as she was concerned. That meant that writing the letter to me was very important to her. I needed to be gracious in receiving it and giving her an acknowledgment that indeed our relationship was what it should be.

How many of us need to write letters like that? What would keep us from doing it? Maybe there is a fear that the person will want to renew animosity. Maybe we hope they have forgotten an unfortunate incident and fear that the letter might rekindle the memory. Just as my former student wrote to me in order to meet her need and not mine, each of us needs to determine if there are similar places in our lives when reaching out to someone would be significant in restoring a broken relationship with someone in this world. The other person might not respond or might even respond in a less than hospitable way. Nonetheless, we will have done what we need to do to be right with a fellow human created by God.

See the Selected Bibliography for further books to read on this subject. The prerequisite here is to feel that you are at peace with both the people and the things around you. Only you know when you have achieved this, but others around will notice it as well.

3. A Desire To Be In Control Of Self

For many of us, the test of success in life comes down to having the basic necessities of life and certain other specific things like a soft chair in front of the TV, a nice car of our choice to drive, air conditioning wherever we go, decent clothes and plenty to eat when we want to eat it. To be in control of ourselves is defined as having these things at our disposal. Some of us are not contented because we always want more material possessions. One person described himself as a "recovering materialist." All of us want some material things. To accomplish much in life we need some things. Our problem comes when we become obsessed with obtaining more toys, more material things. An obsession with material things means that you do not have control over yourself.

Why is self-control so important? Isn't it adequate to be able to say, "I am happy and am enjoying life"? How would you answer that? Let's look at how you can become happy and how you can come to enjoy life.

It is possible to be temporarily happy and feel you are enjoying life by being involved in activities which are contrary to the teachings of the Bible. Persons involved in an extramarital affair convince themselves that they are happy and enjoying life. How many of these people are able to remain happy while in such a relationship? For most of us, this temporary happiness will begin to gnaw at us and cause us to be unhappy. When we seek out short-term happiness which runs counter to our values, it is bound to cause us grief and unhappiness in the long run. To put it another way, long-term happiness comes from behavior and circumstances which are consistent with the value systems we hold.

Long-term happiness, this book suggests, also comes from achieving our thought-out goals which are consistent with the values we hold. Thus, we see that the need to have goals and the need for those goals to be consistent with our personal value systems are essential in our seeking happiness in life.

You can neither set nor achieve goals unless you are in charge of your own life. By being in control of yourself, you are in charge of whether you will be happy as you proceed through life. Not being in control does not mean that someone else is in control. The other option is that there is no control. That means you are simply floating through life accepting whatever happens from the force and initiative of others as well as from your own random behavior. Neither the second alternative (control by others) nor the third one (no control) will lead to long-term happiness. Both alternatives will cause behavior outcomes which are inconsistent with your individual value system and that are costly in many ways to you as a person.

Assuming control of yourself has costs related to it. Being in control means that you must decide what to do with what you control. Being in control does not include an option of doing nothing. The issue is doing what? Doing it when? With what intended effect? Therefore, assuming control of self is a prerequisite to effective personal development.

4. Willingness To Discover Values

Chapter Five has a detailed discussion about discovering, understanding and implementing values. Here we want to introduce the concept that we all have value systems. Although few of us would admire the values of Al Capone, we recognize that he had a value system. In contrast, Billy Graham has a set of highly admired values as indicated in a recent Gallup Poll.[8]

No two people have the same set of values. Values begin to be clarified during the first year of life. They continue to develop throughout life and go through a process of very gradual change. When I was nine, I had a white, metal milk truck I enjoyed playing with on a daily basis. I no longer even have that milk truck. What I do have is a room full of a model railroading layout. And, yes, there are some trucks and cars on that layout. While I don't play with the truck in the sand anymore, I do enjoy building models of vehicles, buildings and railroad equipment. Is there a change in values? Yes, to a degree. Part of our change in values comes from what society expects of us and what we think society will tolerate while maintaining that which we enjoy and are good at doing. Many people might wonder about a man in his fifties who played with trucks in the sand. Some, but not as many, might question his enjoyment of model railroads.

Some of us have unusual interests. These unusual interests might or might not be things that are accepted by society. It takes courage to develop yourself in ways that society questions. One example is the railroad passenger car I bought which then came in on a train to Nashville. Virtually everyone who hears about this railroad car smiles when they hear about it (not everyone hears about it) and then asks the question, "What are you going to do with it?" Do you think this puts some pressure on me relative to this unique interest? It takes some courage to be unique. Yet at the same time, we should never be unique just for the sake of being different.

You might be thinking, hey, wait a minute. Values aren't always determined or even shaped by societal pressure. Right! What else determines our values? They come in part from our abilities, our interests, our circumstances, our experiences, what we are taught, our faith, our friends, and our challenges and opportunities. Because this set of circumstances will be different for each of us, no two of us will have identical sets of values.

We will explore the topic of values further in Chapter Five (Understanding Values: What Is Your Value System?). At this point in the book, I only want to convince you as a reader that there are prerequisites concerning your value system that must be cared for before you can really do something about your own effective personal management. One of them is to wrestle with your value system to determine what it includes and in what priority. Get to know it and be able to realize how it affects everything (**everything**) you do.

5. Willingness To Discover Self And Be That Person

There are two parts to self. One is the inner self. The other is how self relates to others. First let us look at the inner self.

Only you know your inner self. Others see evidence of our inner selves through our behavior and our body language, including facial expressions. But they never come to know it. A husband and wife after many years of marriage only have clues to the inner self of their mate. My parents have been married for seventy-two years and still surprise each other from time to time in what they say or do.

None of us has a full grasp of our own inner selves, and we are sometimes surprised by our thoughts and reactions. This is because of the complexity of the inner self and the limited capacity to fathom all that is stored in the human brain. Knowing what we can about our value systems is a start. Our values dictate much of our thought processes—we think about things we value. Our fears and our desires (what we don't want to happen and what we do want to happen) will dominate much of our thoughts. Our unexpressed thought is the inner self.

Some of us say much of what comes to our minds even without giving it much thought. Those people keep getting into trouble because they vent most of their thoughts and, because their thoughts are still in incubation before being expressed, the verbal expression is half-baked and does not even express what the individual wanted to say.

Others of us seldom speak and then only after thinking through what we should say under the circumstances. Taking this approach will cause people to limit their influence because they hesitate to express their thoughts to others. What they do say might be listened to more, however, if only they had the courage and motivation to speak.

Most of us are in between. We show our inner selves to others some of the time. Our inner selves, however, always have a significant role which is not expressed to anyone else, even a spouse or a close friend. Why is that? Some of it isn't worth expressing. Other thoughts are too private. What keeps thoughts private? The issue in question might be embarrassing (past, present or future), other thoughts might be secret for a reason (Christmas presents on December 23rd, for example), while there might be another interesting area of our private lives that we just prefer to keep private. There seems to be a need in each individual to have a private life. This is a more significant factor with some as compared to others. Having a private life is part of the balance of life—it is the reservoir upon which we can draw, it is the incubator of thoughts not yet ready to be expressed, it is the staging area for ideas to be articulated. These concepts relate to much of the rest of the book, but Chapters Ten and Eleven, in particular, where extending self to others and self-discipline are discussed, will develop these thoughts further.

What has this to do with the prerequisites for effective personal management? What it comes down to is that in order to manage yourself effectively you must have your personal house in order. Part of your personal house is the inner you. You need to have the inner you in a condition that brings you peace and satisfaction in order for you to move to other external, other-person directed activities. Otherwise, the inner you will have problems that will constantly crop up and distract you from other activities. You need to like yourself. When you do to a reasonable degree, you can be pretty sure that your inner self is OK.

What is your attitude like? Are you mad, grumpy or angry much of the time? If so, it is probably directed mostly at the inner self. There are problems there which you need to address. Once you are able to deal with them, you can more effectively deal with a range of other potentials in your life.

6. Willingness To Know And Use Your Spiritual Gifts

There are instruments available for you to discover your spiritual gifts. One of them is the *Gifts Analysis Questionnaire*. Another one is *Team Ministry, A Guide to Spiritual Gifts and Lay Involvement* (Church Growth Institute, P.O. Box 4404, Lynchburg, VA 24502). If you use the second one (*Team Ministry*), you may obtain a Teacher's Guide I adapted from those materials for a four-week use of the materials free of charge from the publisher of this book. Whatever you use; it is important to discover your spiritual gifts.

In the Bible, you might read 1 Corinthians 7:7 to know that we each have at least one gift. First Corinthians 12, Ephesians 4 and Romans 12 are Scriptures you should read again to become more aware of what the Bible says about spiritual gifts. It becomes clear there that God has provided these gifts so that we might use them to further the cause of the Kingdom.

The prerequisite for effective personal management involves getting to know what the Scripture says about spiritual gifts and then determining what to do about the gifts which apply to you. You are not at peace with yourself if you possess a spiritual gift which you are unwilling to develop or use. You must be willing to know (discover) and use your spiritual gifts. It will require effort on your part to discover your gifts, and then an even greater effort to exercise those gifts.

7. Willingness To Set Goals And Follow Them

A willingness to set goals means that you are not satisfied with trying to retain the status quo. You want at least some part of the world to be better. What part of the world, on what timetable and with what resources do you want to bring about change or preserve that which already exists? A goal does not have to represent something different from the present. For example, it could represent maintaining and even building upon a beautiful marriage. Most goals do not start from scratch. There is something desirable in most situations. The goal can be to take a person, place, thing or concept to where it could be, to the fulfillment of your dream. We will return to this subject in Chapter Six.

If you wish to manage yourself effectively, you will have to set goals. Are you ready to do this? Setting goals means writing them down. Goals that remain in your head are not really goals; they are things you are thinking or daydreaming about.

A goal should be more than written, it should also be shown to at least one other person. This says, "I am serious about this goal. I want to accomplish it, and I am willing to do what it takes to make it a reality." The goals do not have to be voluminous. They only have to reflect what you feel is needed to move you toward effective personal management.

8. Willingness To Set Priorities

Solomon was the richest man in the world. He sought to become the happiest man in the world. He could buy anything or any person he wanted. He had many wives. He had whatever the world at that time had to offer. How happy did Solomon become? In the book of Ecclesiastes, Solomon wonders about the meaning of life. He talks about the difficulty of finding meaning in wisdom (Chapters 1 and 2), in pleasure and riches (Chapter 2), in religious practices and the futility of life (Chapter 6), and in Chapter 12 he concluded that we should fear God and keep his commandments.

Solomon had difficulties with establishing priorities. Most of us have so many earthly goods and so many opportunities that it is difficult for us to sort out what is most important. Unless we know what is most important, we don't know where to start, where to act. While many things are important, what is really most important right now? What should be demanding my attention at this minute? Note that at this moment the highest priority might not be an earthshaking event. Maybe right now the priority is to go take the clothes out of the dryer. That is a matter of time priority, of determining what should be addressed first, then second and third.

Then there is significance priority. What is really significant in my life? Am I devoting enough attention to these matters. While we do need to take the clothes out of the dryer when they are done, we have lost sight of significance priority if we spend all day every day dealing with items of similar significance. To give loving attention to a child and to take clothes out of a dryer are both important and both will have a time when it is best to give attention to them. However, loving a child, our values will tell us, has a much higher significance priority. We must order our lives so that the items of greatest significance priority will get adequate attention.

The prerequisite here is that in order to have effective personal management we must be willing to set time priorities and significance priorities. Are you willing to do this?

9. Willingness To Learn (have to choose to learn)

We used to have the notion in our society that formal education ended at about twenty-two for the best educated males and much earlier for the rest of us, depending upon whether we went beyond grammar school (later elementary school) and then high school (a phenomena of the last hundred years). Now the idea is that formal learning goes on forever, and we have increasingly sophisticated devices to enable us to continue that process. Credit and noncredit courses offered by colleges and technical schools, completion of high school in the evening and learning at home through correspondence or television are just some of the opportunities we have for formal learning. As a result, a much higher percentage of people today are continuing their formal education.

Likewise, informal education, that which we pick up from listening and observing as we progress through life, never ends although some people try to shut it out of their lives. Some of this has an effect upon us that we cannot avoid. Some of it we seek out when we buy an interesting nonfiction book.

Seeking out learning is essential to prepare us for the rapid changes in the world today. If we do not continue to learn, we leave our fates increasingly to those others who do know what is happening. Thus we lose our opportunities to effectively manage ourselves.

Only by continuing to learn (what Stephen Covey calls "sharpening the saw"[9]), do we have the opportunity to maintain or improve our positions. The prerequisite here for effective personal management is that we must have an attitude which says, "I want to continue to learn and I will find opportunities to make that happen."

10. Courage—Willingness To Risk

Some of us like to look at the mail and read the letters that tell us that we have just won $25,000. In the fine print we find that our names are only one among a list of many people who might win and that to keep our names in this pool we have to take a certain action which might include buying something. This is an approach of waiting for our "ship to come in" (as my father would humorously tell us when we were children and we felt we had to have some nonessential item). Sometimes others do take care of us, particularly in a time of considerable need. But waiting for others to help us reach our goals means we have little or no control over whether or not we will reach our goals. We also have little control over whether we will have effective personal management.

To be in control of our lives, we must be willing to take some risk and to exercise courage. The greater the risk, the greater the amount of courage required to be in control. If our goals are modest, little courage will be required to make them a reality. If, on the other hand, our goals are ambitious, then much risk taking will be required. The thirty- or forty-year-old man who decides to leave his line of work to go to Bible college so that he might enter some form of Christian service is taking a risk. Maybe he won't do well in Bible college. Maybe the new career after he finishes college will not be satisfying or maybe there won't be one right away. Leaving a secure job and a comfortable home is certainly a risk.

In order to have effective personal management, we must be willing to take risks (demonstrate courage) commensurate with the goals we have set and the priorities associated with those goals. Assuming that you have your goals written down and your priorities worked through, what risks will you have to take in order to make those goals a reality? Are you willing to take those risks?

11. Willingness To Act Consistently Over A Long Period Of Time

Being willing to act consistently over a long period of time gives you the opportunity to develop incrementally and achieve goals that are themselves consistent with one another. Reputations can be destroyed in an instant. Reputations are built over a long period of time and the longer they have developed, the more reliable the reputation is considered to be.

We gain personal confidence from being able to act consistently in a positive way over a period of time. It is an accomplishment. There are many times when we can fall. If we have not fallen for a long period of time, it is something to be admired. Such is the basis for the platform needed to have effective personal management.

You might respond by saying, "Look, I'm a new Christian and I have not acted consistently over a period of time. So what do I do?" The answer is that you have already taken the first step—getting started in the right direction based upon a Christian faith and a strong set of values. Now you can start down the long road of consistency. But it does not mean you have to just sit tight and do nothing for many years. In fact, those with a great reputation have earned it by **doing** much over the many years. So get busy doing. Doing what, you say? Go to your goals. Set some strategies of how to accomplish those goals, and then set a priority of what you will do right now. Yes, right now. Don't put it off until tomorrow. Start the long path of consistent behavior as soon as possible.

12. Willingness To Assume Responsibility—To Be In Charge Of Your Future

All of this is a prelude to recognizing that when all is said and done, it's up to you to make it happen. That is the process of accepting responsibility. When you accept responsibility, you will take the necessary initiative rather than wait for others to do things for you.

It is awesome to recognize that you are in charge of your future. God will help, but you must initiate the changes. Are you ready to begin, to take control by setting goals, to develop strategies for accomplishing them and to set priorities to determine what happens next?

Conclusion

Throughout this chapter you should have felt challenged regardless of where you are on the scale toward effective personal management. Those who have made a lot of progress might have identified with even more of the concepts because they are more conscious of their importance.

The assumptions discussed here are given as the basis for the entire book. You might refer back to them from time to time to refresh your memory.

The prerequisites are the beginning of a system in which you, the reader, are given a handle on how to manage your own life effectively. Possibly you have mastered them all. If so, congratulations. You now have the opportunity to help others. If not, get out a pad of paper and begin to develop a plan of what you will do in order to meet each prerequisite fully.

Endnotes

[1]"Wives, submit to your husbands as to the Lord. For the husband is the head of the wife as Christ is the head of the church, his body, of which he is the Savior. Now as the church submits to Christ, so also wives should submit to their husbands in everything" (Eph. 5:22).

[2]"You are all sons of God through faith in Christ Jesus, for all of you who were baptized into Christ have clothed yourselves with Christ. There is neither Jew nor Greek, slave nor free, male nor female, for you are all one in Christ Jesus" (Gal. 3:26-28).

[3]1 Corinthians 13:1-13. See also 1 John 5:2-4, "This is how we know that we love the children of God: by loving God and carrying out his commands. This is love for God: to obey his commands. And his commands are not burdensome, for everyone born of God overcomes the world. This is the victory that has overcome the world, even our faith."

[4]Romans 12:1-2.

[5]1 Thessalonians 5:17.

[6]2 Timothy 2:15.

[7]Hebrews 10:25.

[8]According to information on the Billy Graham Evangelistic Association home page, Dr. Graham has placed among the "Ten Most Admired Men in the World" from the Gallup Poll a total of 37 times since 1955. His list of awards and honors is both long and impressive.

[9]Stephen R. Covey, *The Seven Habits of Highly Effective People: Restoring the Character Ethic* (New York, NY: Simon and Schuster, 1989), pp. 287ff.

Chapter Two

Who Am I? Know Yourself

To achieve excellence there must first be knowledge, experience and perspective. The first area of knowledge must begin with self. It is here that we start to understand our own world. —Kenneth W. Oosting

Knowing Yourself

n this chapter we will **first** look at who we have been, our past. This past has both a reality and our perception of that reality. The two are not the same. Our ability to cope is partially dependent upon our success in keeping the two closely identified.

The **second** view in this chapter will be to look at who we are now. The past has led us to our present condition. We have the opportunity to be more accurate with this perception because it is based partly on current feedback from others (one of the ways we assess who we are).

The **third** view in this chapter is of who we want to be. In this perception there is only one set of facts unless we ourselves are deluded (all of us are to some extent). These are our dreams.

The **fourth** adds a touch of realism to the third view and asks who we are likely to become. Our dreams are limited by our ambition, our willingness to make sacrifices, our willingness to work, our leadership, our health, the support of others and God's will for our lives.

We can pause at any point in life to reflect on who we have been, who we are now and who we hope to be. Our reflection is likely to be riddled with rationalization and unwillingness to look realistically at certain areas of life (indeed, there are parts of our lives we cannot evaluate realistically because we have so much emotional baggage connected with those events or periods). Nevertheless, it could be helpful to do what we can and are willing to do in looking at ourselves. After all, others do it every day and they come up with conclusions about us based upon what they see and experience. Since our success in life is related to how others see us, we should know how others see us. How they see us begins with their picture of who we have been (at times that picture is so strong that it clouds the real picture of who we are today). So let's first ask, "Who have I been?"

Who Have I Been?

As a historian, I tend to look first at the history of a person or organization in order to understand who or what they are in the present. The past is really a great predictor of the present and the future. This is because the talents we have now, the values we have now, the goals we have now and the ambitions we currently hold all have roots in the past. While it is true that they might be slightly different today from yesterday and there might be a growing gap between the past and today, it is still true that the talents, values, goals and ambitions that we have gradually evolve throughout life unless some event (such as the loss of a loved one, loss of a job or a religious conversion) brings about a major change. Few of us ever go through a major change overnight. Our recent past is almost always a sure predictor of what we are today.

So, in order to understand yourself, you must first begin with answering the question of who you have been. It has been said that the best way to determine your values, the things really important in your life, is to look at two books: your appointment book (or a logbook of time) and your checkbook. These tell how you have used your precious commodities of time and money. Further, they are easily measured. Each day has twenty-four hours. How did you use them? Your income tax forms tell how much money came to you in a year. Your checkbooks and bank statements tell you how you have spent your money more recently. How did you spend it?

Likewise, you have a given amount of time. How much do you spend in sleeping? in watching television? in other leisure activities? The critical factor is the correlation between the discretionary time you have and your goals. Your discretionary time is what is left after you deduct your normal sleeping time (usually seven to eight hours, not ten hours unless you have medical problems), your work time, your time to get to and from work and a minimal time to eat (some of us elect to spend a considerable amount of our discretionary time in eating). How much time is left?

You can't save time. You spend what you have every day. Look at yesterday, your last full twenty-four hour period. Where did the discretionary time get spent? Be honest with yourself. Don't confuse discretionary time with what was required of you. If you took ninety minutes or two hours for your evening meal, how much of that was discretionary time?

What do you have to show for your time and money? You make many decisions in the spending of your time and money. Those decisions are a reflection of your values. You will spend both your money and your time inevitably, but how you spend them is up to you personally. You might blame others in order to shift the responsibility from yourself, but how these two resources are spent is still largely up to you.

To explore how you have managed your financial resources, do a thorough analysis of what your resources were during the past twelve months (income, gifts, tax refunds and your time resource) and then categorize the groups of time and money expenditures. Try to avoid rationalizing. Instead, use a typical financial budget for your type of household. Use a similar tactic to measure how you spent your time. Using the standard categories, analyze the expenditures from your cash and credit cards to see how each expenditure was made. Many who complete this exercise will find that their expenditures are different than they previously thought.

You might say that you can't spend your time and money the way that you want to because you must care for your elderly mother or your children are chronically ill and require much of your time and your money. Then there is the issue that you have very little discretionary time or money in your life because the necessities take up all your money and everyone demands all your time. Does any of this sound like you?

What are your necessities? Does everyone demand your time or do you freely (and maybe begrudgingly) give it away? Who is in control of your life? We will return to this issue of being in control of your life during later chapters.

At this point I am going to ask you to complete an exercise. In the exercise on the following pages, you are asked to think about how you have spent your time and money and other life resources so far. As you complete this exercise, take some time to think about your past and to reflect upon what you really did and what you really valued.

The outcome might not be the picture you currently have of yourself. Hopefully, this exercise will cause you to think differently about the present and the future. Now move to the exercise. When you have completed it, return to the paragraph which follows it and we will discuss what you discovered. Because this is very personal, you might want to record your answers in a notebook rather than in this book.

AN INVENTORY OF MY PAST

To make this an inventory of your past, I suggest that you take a day in your life that was approximately 365 days ago and answer the questions from the vantage point of that day. To be sure, you will have to guess at some of the facts. However, if you have a diary or an appointment book, consult it. If that particular day was very unusual, pick another one prior to that date.

To get the full effect of responding to this exercise, **you must write down** your responses. Record them on a separate piece of paper and keep it where it will remain confidential. After you have finished reading this book, you could either store the responses away in a secure place to examine later or add to (or correct) or you could discard them. Do not discard them, however, before you finish reading this book.

MY CHILDHOOD
  Was my childhood happy?
  Do I have good memories from it?
  Record one or more such good memories.
  Do I like to talk about (think about) that period in my life?

MY PARENTS
  Were my parents loving—did they care about me?
  Do I like to talk about/with my parents today?
  Are there stories that are indicative of my parental rela-
    tionship?
  If so, write down one of those stories.

MY FAVORITE THINGS I HAVE DONE
  What did I do?
  How old was I?
  What made the event(s) memorable?

THE PAST EVENT(S) OF WHICH I AM THE PROUDEST
  What did I do in three of my proudest moments?
  How old was I?

Why am I proud of this event?
Did others notice this event?

THE DARKEST PART OF MY LIFE
What happened?
What caused it?
How am I dealing with it? Does it still affect me? How?

ANY TRAUMATIC EVENTS?
What happened?
What caused it?
How have I felt about it since that time?
What have I done about it since that time?
How am I dealing with it? Does it still affect me? How?

TO WHAT EXTENT HAS MY LIFE SO FAR BEEN DIRECTED BY GOALS?
To what extent were those goals written?
To what extent did I act in accordance with those goals? (self-discipline)
What has been the impact of having goals and following them?

TO WHAT EXTENT HAVE I BEEN ABLE TO SET PRIORITIES SO FAR IN MY LIFE?
Have these priorities been written?
Have I paid attention to them?
Have they had an impact on my life?
Do I control and set these priorities or are they set by others?

HOW DID I SPEND THE DAY 365 DAYS AGO?
Sleeping?
Eating?
Traveling including to/from work?
Working?
Spending time with family?
Enjoying leisure projects?
Working on other projects such as home repair?

Being a couch potato/watching TV?
How much was spent on self vs. others?

HOW AM I DOING ON MY CAREER GOALS?
What are my career goals?
What progress have I made on these goals in the past twenty-four months?
How do I feel about my progress to date?

HAVE I MANAGED TO SPEND LESS THAN I MAKE?
How much of what I have spent has been for actual essentials? (the things everyone buys)
How much has been discretionary?
What have I done with discretionary income?
    Hobbies
    Additional food
    Cigarettes, alcohol, candy
    Cars
    House, furniture
    Travel
    Donations including helping others
    Other
How much have I saved/invested in the past?
Has my saving/investment been regular over the years?

WHAT HAS MY ATTITUDE TOWARD LIFE BEEN?
How much has it changed over the years?
How do I treat others?
How much of the time am I grumpy or cross?
How much of my time has gone to help others?

DO I HAVE DISCRETIONARY TIME TO DO WHAT I WANT TO DO?
Do I know what I want to do in discretionary time?
How much discretionary time do I really have?
How do I feel about my use of discretionary time?
What am I going to do in the next month that I did not do in the past month?

WHAT ARE MY THOUGHTS ABOUT THE ABOVE?
    After going through this exercise, what thoughts really stick
       out?
    Why do you think these thoughts are dominant?

Now you have completed the exercise about your past. Be
sure that you wrote down your answers. Just reading through
the questions without writing down your answers allows you
to avoid really answering tough questions.

Recording your answers probably caused you to think about
a number of things you have not thought about for some time.
Are you happy with who you have been? If your answer is
yes, you are more likely to have positive feelings about who
you are today and who you will become.

Regardless, there is no way to change what happened in
the past and there is much you can do about the present and
future. There are, however, things you can do about how you
feel about the past. If a past event colors how you view the
present and future, you should really deal with that feeling
now. Obtain professional help if necessary.

How can the past be a learning platform for the present
and future? If negative things about the past still bother us or
keep the present from being as pleasant as it could be, what
are we going to do to put these things to rest, to put them
behind us? Often people are limited in the present and future
by their view about their past. We must get beyond the place
that the past is an anchor which holds us to where we are.
We must pull up the anchor and be ready to put it down in
new water where our charts have taken us. Only we ourselves can control our lives. Is that what we want to do? If so,
let's do it. But before we design the future, let's look at the
present to see what else we can learn there.

For most of us, the past is a real springboard to the present
and future. Allow it to do this for you. Recalling positive
things about the past, even revisiting places and people who
were significant in your past (such as a former teacher who
had a positive effect on you, an uncle or aunt, your parents)
can bring to mind many positive things about your past. This

can help you feel good about who you have been and put the whole of that experience in perspective.

Who Am I Today?

The ancient philosopher Socrates once said to his follow-ers, "Know Yourself." Why would he have made such a state-ment? Obviously we all know our names, our addresses, our phone numbers and many other essential things about our current lives that enable us to negotiate life each day. What does "Know Yourself" mean beyond these many pieces of in-formation that we use each day?

To look at who we have been can be determined largely by facts. Each of us can dream about who we want to be. It is more difficult to determine who we are today.

Putting an emphasis on knowing yourself suggests that there is more to you than what others see on the surface. What is the real you and what kind of person do others perceive you to be? To an extent you are what others and you personally *think* you are. So what is that? How can you find out?

Maybe you don't really want to know because of what it will reveal. Even how you feel about learning about yourself tells a great deal about your level of self-confidence (and the larger view of self-worth) as well as your appraisal of what you have contributed in life to date.

How should you proceed in your journey of self-discovery? What is self anyway? Are each of us really different in our makeup or have we become different simply due to different experiences in our lives?

Perceiving Reality

What is the difference between the way you perceive yourself and how others see you? We do know that there is a difference between reality, self-perception and how others perceive us. In fact, each person perceives another in his or her own way. None of the perceptions, by others or by ourselves, is accurate (completely in keeping with reality). We need to stay in touch with reality, while at the same time we remember that it is not possible to achieve a goal of matching self-perception with reality. So how do we relate reality to at least two perceptions of that reality?

As long as we understand that perceptions of reality and reality itself will never come together, we can only work at keeping the gap between them manageable by constantly being in a position in which we examine both the reality and the perceptions. This is challenging the perceptions of others. How do we challenge each others' perceptions? We do it by testing it against reality. When we get too far from reality we are challenged by others.

Another way to test our perception of reality is to review our behavior. If our behavior is very different from the behavior of others and others begin to complain about our behavior or place certain penalties on this behavior, it is possible that we are lengthening our gap between reality and our perception of reality.

Talking with friends, particularly close friends, can give us a reality check. Do we understand them? Do we often agree with them? Are we changing our relationships with long time friends?

Learning About Self

We have two options in learning about ourselves. We can do it in the overall view of who we are, or we can look at ourselves through the microscope by examining all the individual pieces. Let's take the overall view first. To examine ourselves overall we might ask such questions as the following:

1. How am I different from others? (Think about what happens inside you and how this manifests itself in your behavior.)

2. What do I believe in — do I have a Christian faith? (If so, take out a piece of paper and write out a description of

your faith in a quarter page to a full page. If you can't write it out or have someone else write it for you, your faith is probably quite shallow and does not have much effect on you and others. If you cannot keep it to one page, then you have a different problem in sorting out the essentials from the examples and finer points of your faith.) Is my faith clear enough and strong enough that I could lead another person to Christ?

3. Does my faith affect my daily life today? If it does, give three examples of action in the past three days.

4. Do I have goals? Are there things I want to accomplish in life? If so, what are they? Do I already have a list? (If so, review it now before proceeding on with the rest of the book. If you have no list, this is a good time to start one. Putting your goals on paper forces you to think them through in a manner that you can more easily understand a year later when you pick up the paper.) The written goal is more focused, more complete. The written goal also becomes more of a commitment. The obvious next question after writing a goal is what now will I do about reaching this goal?

5. Do I have priorities? (It is good to have goals but you can't accomplish them all at the same time unless your goals are unusually simple. This requires the setting of priorities.) What is most important? What do I need to do right now? What about later today? What about tomorrow and next week? (Interesting people have goals and priorities because those goals and priorities themselves are probably interesting. Dull people simply go through a day because the day is there and they do not know what else to do. Being interesting is not a matter of intelligence either. Some mentally limited people are very interesting. Some very bright people are extremely dull.)

6. What interesting thing(s) am I currently doing in my life? (It need not be a major event. It could be planting a flower garden. It could be reading a book which is causing you to think. It could be as major as going through a soul-searching process of trying to define your Christian faith.)

7. What do others think of me? What terms do they use to describe me? To what extent am I comfortable with those terms?

8. What have I done during the past year to make this a better world? Do I even have an idea of how to make this a better world? Do I have an interest in helping to improve life for others? If so, what have I done recently to carry out this interest? (Be specific. If the list is long, congratulations. If you can't think of anything to put on the list, are you sure you have the interest or is this something you wish others would do?)

9. What do I think of myself? Do I put myself down for things I do? How do I walk? (People reveal a lot about their self-esteems by how they walk, how they carry themselves.) What am I capable of doing? Does anyone want me to do those things? Am I currently doing those things? What do I think, really think, about life and its meaning, about my relationship to Christ and about what is really important in this world? Do I like myself? Can others tell this by my behavior? Am I generally happy?

The two most important things about us currently are our values (including our Christian faith) and our attitudes (including what we intend to do to act on our values). Chapter Five is devoted to the issue of understanding values and helping you to discover your own value system. Learning about your value system will assist you in knowing much about who you have been, who you are now, who you want to be and what is likely to actually happen in your life. One of the best places to start in discovering your value system is with an inventory of who you are right now. Your most important inventory is not about what car you drive or even who your friends are. It begins with what your value system is. What spiritual and secular things and concepts are important to you? What is their relationship to each other (obviously some things are much more important than others)? What is a value anyway? A value is something you hold dear and use to determine what behavior you should engage in during your life.

Who Do I Want To Be?

Now that we have looked at who we have been and who we are now, the third step is to consider who we want to become. The future will bring about change in our lives whether or not we favor that change. So the alternative of keeping our lives the same until we die is not an option. We can decide that we will not initiate any change, but we still have to determine how we will react to the external change that we cannot control.

The best way to react to external change is to be proactive. To be proactive means that you favor action and will initiate it in ways that correspond with your values and goals. An example is inflation. To be inactive is to simply pay more for what you want in the future because external factors have caused prices to go up as a result of inflation. To be proactive is to look at inflation and, while recognizing that you cannot control it, to decide what action you will take in order to turn inflation to an advantage. One method might be buying land that will go up in value with inflation rather than buying a car which will have a resale value positively affected by inflation but to a minor extent. To do so is to be proactive. That is, to decide what your future will be within the alternatives you have in life. Control the things you can in order to minimize the effects of negative factors you cannot control.

It is always better to be proactive. But to be proactive requires the expenditure of energy. You have to do something. You have to have goals, strategies for those goals and priorities of what to do next. Change in our society is occurring at an unprecedented rate. Expansion of knowledge and advances in technology are causing our society to change rapidly. We cannot even look at our fathers and grandfathers and say we would like to have lives like theirs. Much of what was true in their lives will not be true in our futures, even if we proactively try to make it happen. Life will be different in the future, but this only increases the options as unknowns multiply in the mix of factors influencing our futures.

To be proactive in regard to your future is essential. To be proactive, you must have goals, strategies to achieve those goals and priorities for determining what requires your action now and later. This gives you something to be proactive toward. The two go together. To have goals, strategies and priorities without being proactive means only that you have a wish list that someone else might bring about. To be proactive without goals is to act in many areas with any positive results being accidental.

There are many things wrong with the world in which we live (as has been true of the world ever since Adam and Eve), and there will be problems in the world in the future until the second coming of Christ. We must accept this lack of perfection in the world and use it as an opportunity to do something which will improve the world around us rather than saying the world is so corrupt that it is not worth our effort. Such a view is rationalization. God created this world. It is not up to you and me to evaluate it and determine that He did not do a very good job. God created us as well and He created us to be in this world. We are given more opportunities than we can ever act upon in one lifetime. What we need to do is get busy with the opportunities at hand and with the portion of our lives that remains to accomplish some of what God has given us the challenge and the opportunity to address. To help us address those issues He gave us talents, time and other resources along with a mind to figure out how to put all these resources together toward a positive outcome.

Did you ever consider why God did not create a perfect world for us to live in? While the Garden of Eden was close to perfect, it did contain the serpent and thus temptation. The Garden of Eden represents opportunity and resources while Adam and Eve represent each person in the world who has a free will to either obey God, disobey God or ignore Him. He lets us make the choice. The Bible is quite clear about the rewards and penalties of our behavior within those choices that we have a free will to make. Nevertheless, God has allowed us to create a society of our choice. The society we have is the one we and our fellow men created. Each of us is an individual in this society and thus we have the same basic opportunity to affect the world. As the New Testament describes, we are created with different abilities and talents. One of those is leadership. As a result, some of us are in a better position to lead the world toward making the society a better one. However, all of us, every one of us, have an opportunity to make a contribution not only to make society a better one but also to become the chief architect in designing our own lives — in determining who we will become. How willing are you to be the architect of your own life?

To be that architect requires energy (God gave you that), time (God gave you that), physical resources such as a home (God gave you that), friends (God gave you choices), opportunities (God gave you that) and goals (you furnish that). What are your goals? Chapter Six is devoted to setting goals and helps you address the question of what you want to happen? The most important of these goals is related to who YOU will become. God furnishes the time and materials; it is up to you to be the workman to use the time and materials to create that which will bring honor and glory to His Kingdom.

Who Will I Become?

In this chapter we have been looking at:

- WHO HAVE I BEEN?

- WHO AM I NOW?

- WHO DO I WANT TO BE?

And now we will look at:

- WHO WILL I BECOME?

The answers to the prior questions can be found by looking at your past (question one), your present (question two) and your future (question three). The fourth question is not the same as question three, although it might appear to be at first glance.

The last question was "Who do I want to be?" That involves looking into the future, making plans, setting priorities. The question "Who will I become?" asks a little different question. The difference can be found in:

- the clarity of my goals in stating what I wish to become,
- the strength of my motivation to achieve "who I want to become,"
- my talents and abilities as well as how those talents match up with who I want to become,
- some element of chance, and
- the sacrifices I am willing to make.

As you walk through a cemetery you can wonder how many of the people buried there achieved the goals they set out for themselves. How many of them became what they sought to become? Probably not many. Why not? Study the list above related to others and yourself. What is the clarity of your goals? What is the strength of your motivation? Do you have the talents and abilities needed for your goals? What sacrifices are you willing to make on a continuous basis? What about others you know?

None of us can affect the past or even the present. You can alter how you feel about those times but not the times themselves. From the viewpoint of the present, it might be good to ask how you might achieve a greater percentage of your goals than the people mentioned above who have markers in cemeteries with their names on them. What can you do today to increase the likelihood that your goals will be reached? The following suggestions for action today can help bring about the future that you want to have.

1. Go off by yourself with a pad of paper and a pen to a quiet place where you will not be distracted by others or a telephone and without time pressures so that you can expand the time if you are finding it profitable. Become comfortable and make a dream list of what you would like to see happen in your lifetime. This should include personal things, items relating to family, to work, to community and on behalf of society. At this point just sketch a few words that will remind you of the thought later. The following space could be used to make some notes. It is important to bring clarity to these goals although you might not be able to do so at this sitting. The clearer, more specific your goals are, the more likely that you will have a clear picture in your mind which will lead to increased likelihood of goal accomplishment.

GOAL NUMBER ONE

GOAL NUMBER TWO

GOAL NUMBER THREE

GOAL NUMBER FOUR

GOAL NUMBER FIVE

(Add numbers so that there is space for each of your goals.)

2. The next step might be to share the list with those close to you and whose advice and counsel you respect. Paul Tournier in his book, *To Understand Each Other*, makes the comment about the strategy of discovering oneself that:

No one comes to know himself through introspection, or in the solitude of his personal diary. Rather, it is in dialogue, in his meeting with other persons. It is only by expressing his convictions to others that he becomes really conscious of them. He who would see himself clearly must open up to a confidant freely chosen and worthy of such trust.[1]

A discussion of this type will help you refine the list by establishing which goals are really important to you. This process will eliminate the goals, even though they are worthy goals, that fail to capture your interest. The number of items on the final list depends on your energy, talent, sacrifices you are willing to make and, most of all, drive (how badly you want it to happen).

3. If you can't visualize a goal, you probably can't make it happen. Visualizing it allows you to think through the various implications of a goal. If you can't visualize it, you don't have a clear enough picture of what it is that you wish to happen. Give it some more thought. Very global thoughts, like ending world hunger, that you cannot visualize probably belong to the category of goals (described in number three above) that you are not likely to devote sufficient energy to achieve. Now, on the other hand, if you can visualize eradicating hunger in your town or in some far away place and have some ideas about how to make it happen, then your goal becomes a possibility.

4. Now refine the list. Include only those things that you are willing to commit time and energy to make happen, those things that you are willing to make the necessary sacrifices to realize and those things you are able to visualize. To be on your list of goals, an item must meet these criteria. Now, how many are still on the list?

5. A goal must have a strategy. How will you make this happen? What action will you take (and encourage others to

take) that will bring your goal closer to happening? Many strategies will need supporting strategies. If a strategy is to go see a particular person, your substrategy will include transportation, funding, timing and other related items.

6. What priority is the accomplishment of these goals in your life? Are you willing to devote time and energy to a goal right now? Next year? Five years from now? Maybe a small amount of time and energy now and greater amounts later? Look at your time and energy as the cost of making the goal happen. Just as you cannot buy something without giving something for it, you must give something to achieve a goal. Giving something often means sacrificing something else. This brings us back to priorities. What are the priorities in your life?

7. Successful people are busy people. They find time to do things when others see no time available. A successful person controls his time rather than being controlled by time. What do you want to do, how much time will it realistically take and what other resources must be present? The basic question is, how effectively can you use your time? We all have the same amount. Can you get more from your time than most others do? Are you willing to make commitments to yourself and others about what you will accomplish in a given amount of time on a specific project? Are you willing to make sacrifices? Be realistic, but make commitments. Then organize yourself to meet your commitments.

8. Be of courage. Thomas Aquinas spoke of courage as a strength of the mind which renders man capable of accomplishing that which he considers the highest good, the highest value.[2] Now we know that other factors—such as talent, financial and other resources, having clear goals, sacrifices and time—influence whether we reach the highest attainment of our goals. However, most of us are not realistically limited by talent, resources and time; we find

ways to conquer those things. There are too many success stories such as that of Wilma Rudolph who could not walk, but who later became an Olympic runner. We tend to be limited more by our lack of courage to attain the goals we seek than by any other factor. Think through your courage barriers and attack them individually in order to increase your courage to attain the goals that are important to you. More will be said about courage later in the book.

After I set the goal of writing this book, I discovered that I had set an unrealistic timetable for its completion because of other projects I have that demand my time and attention. The timetable changed, but my goal to finish the book did not change. It must get done was my thought. This was my commitment to myself and to others (including the colleges where it is to be a textbook). Living up to a commitment can be difficult, but it sorts out your priorities and reminds you that you must allocate certain amounts of time and energy to do that to which you have committed yourself.

One of the saddest thoughts in life is to reach the time when life appears to be nearing the end only to have regrets about not having set goals, not having lived the lives we feel we should have lived. When Mickey Mantle died recently, he spoke to the youth of today and said, don't do what I did. The only way to avoid regrets later in life—that life did not turn out as you wanted—is to set goals now (regardless of whether you are 14, 38, 65 or 95) and then begin to accomplish what is important in the time that remains in your life.

Now is the time to take action in your life.

Endnote

[1] Paul Tournier, *To Understand Each Other* (Atlanta, GA: John Knox Press, 1974), p. 30.

[2] Thomas Aquinas, *Summa Theologiae*, 2. 2. 139. 1 and 2.

Chapter Three

What Does It Mean To Be A Christian?

For God so loved the world that he gave his one and only Son, that whoever believes in him shall not perish but have eternal life – John 3:16

You might be considering the question of why deal with the topic of what it means to be a Christian in a book on effective personal development. The answer to that question, even if you had not intended to ask it, is that the book is a "Christian's Guide." As a result, the audience is the Christian. A barrier for the person who claims Christianity but is not sure what it means to be a Christian is the issue of what behavior is appropriate and what is required of a Christian. To be personally effective as a Christian, you must understand Christianity and the commitments it requires. In this chapter we will consider the basics of who God is, what Christianity represents and its impact upon the Christian in his or her own personal development.

Who Is God?

J. I. Packer, Professor at Regent College in Vancouver, British Columbia, Canada, in his book, *Knowing God*, in introducing the concept of why we need to know God suggests that:

> A study of the nature and character of God...is the most practical project anyone can engage in. Knowing about God is crucially important for the living of our lives. As it would be cruel to an Amazonian tribesman to fly him to London, put him down without explanation in Trafalgar Square and leave him, as one who knew nothing of English or England, to fend for himself, so we are cruel to ourselves if we try to live in this world without knowing about the God whose world it is and who runs it. The world becomes a strange, mad, painful place, and life in it a disappointing and unpleasant business, for those who do not know about God. Disregard the study of God, and you sentence yourself to stumble and blunder through life blindfolded, as it were, with no sense of direction and no understanding of what surrounds you. This way you can waste your life and lose your soul.[1]

You might question, "Isn't this overstating the case?" How will I "waste" my life and "lose" my soul by not knowing God? You might add that you have some knowledge of God and that understanding God, after all, is beyond human comprehension. Someone might contribute to this by saying that we have theologians who devote their life to understanding God and we can rely upon them to tell us anything we need to know.

What do we need to know about God? Packer suggests there are five basic truths about God:

1. God has spoken to man, and the Bible is his Word, given to us to make us wise unto salvation.

2. God is Lord and King over his world; he rules all things for his own glory, displaying his perfections in all that he

does, in order that men and angels may worship and adore him.

3. God is Savior, active in sovereign love through the Lord Jesus Christ to rescue believers from the guilt and power of sin, to adopt them as his children and to bless them accordingly.

4. God is triune; there are within the Godhead three persons, the Father, the Son and the Holy Spirit; and the work of salvation is one in which all three act together, the Father proposing redemption, the Son securing it and the Spirit applying it.

5. Godliness means responding to God's revelation in trust and obedience, faith and worship, prayer and praise, submission and service. Life must be seen and lived in the light of God's Word. This, and nothing else, is true religion.[2]

Do you know God? Is God a partner in your life? Do you communicate with God through prayer on a daily basis? What are you going to do about any of your answers to these questions which you recognize as unsatisfactory?

The vehicles for knowing God are prayer and Bible study (either alone or with others). Prayer and study, however, often do not occur without a plan and a commitment to that plan. It is suggested here that you buy the Packer book mentioned above and read it while at the same time reading through the Bible. Interspersed in this study should be daily prayer. "And my God will meet all your needs according to his glorious riches in Christ Jesus" (Phil. 4:19).

What Is Christianity?

Now if you know God, does that make you a Christian? Satan **knows** God. The New Testament chronicles the birth of

Jesus Christ, His life on earth and His death on the cross. It also makes it clear as to what is required to be a Christian.

Christianity is, in essence, a faith that is described in John 3:16: "For God so loved the world that he gave his one and only Son, that whoever believes in him shall not perish but have eternal life." Christianity says there is an omnipotent God who sent His son to this earth to live among men and die to save man from His sins if man will only believe in God. Salvation, then, provides that man will go to heaven instead of hell at the time of departure from this earth. Salvation is freely offered to all persons, but each individual person must decide to accept the gift. We are expected to live Christlike lives after we acknowledge our belief in Him and to follow other precepts in the Bible about the Christian life, including efforts to win others over to faith in Him.

There is much more to Christianity. But this is it in essence. Man must decide whether to accept or reject Christ. Because we are given a free will to make choices in life, there will be some who accept this salvation and go to heaven when they leave this earth. Others will reject the faith and suffer the consequences in the life to come.

Christians will have questions. LeRoy Lawson, in his book *Questions For God,* devotes a chapter to each of these ten different questions we have.[3] They are:

1. Why is there suffering in the world?

2. Will there ever be a cure for all diseases?

3. Why is there evil in the world?

4. Will there ever be lasting world peace?

5. Will man ever love his fellow man?

6. When will the world end?

7. What does the future hold?

8. Is there life after death?

9. What is heaven like?

10. How can I be a better person?

Christian faith is based in part upon fact. There is factual proof that Jesus lived. Many of the events described in the Bible can be supported by historical evidence while no part of the Bible can be disproved by the evidence. Yet there is the "leap of faith" that is the core of Christian faith. We cannot be Christians based upon historical evidence alone. We must take the "leap of faith" and say, "I believe and as a result of my belief I will do as God commands me." God purposely does not force us to believe, yet He gives us the opportunity to believe.

Because we have a free will on this earth and we live in a complex world, there are many pitfalls where we can go wrong. We cannot say "I believe" one day and let that suffice for the remainder of our lives any more than we can say to a spouse "I love you" once and assume that it need not be reaffirmed. We are given the Bible and Christian fellowship and worship to constantly bring us closer to God and to a fuller understanding of what it means to be a Christian. Steve Douglass writes about "Let the Bible Keep You Out of Trouble."[4] He goes on to write about a person who was a Christian but had goals inconsistent with that faith.[5] The Bible becomes the definitive guide for the Christian when what he or she wants conflicts with God's Word.

Alexander Campbell, a religious leader of the nineteenth century who called for all Christians to join together, argued for the centrality of the Bible as the "sole, exclusive and ultimate source of morality."[6] Campbell went on to warn against authority within the church that would replace the authority of the Bible, a practice he saw growing within Protestantism just as it had earlier in the Catholic church. The message here is that the Bible is the final source of authority for guidance in our Christianity, not any preaching or written document.

It is in the New Testament that we receive the greatest amount of guidance about what it means to be a Christian. The Epistles of Paul, in particular, are helpful to us. Because Paul tried to guide the early Christians in what it meant to be a Christian, we have the advantage of reading his letters and can apply much of it directly to our own churches and our personal lives. The Book of James is devoted to issues of practical Christian living. James, for example, deals with such topics as the unbridled tongue, the test of brotherly love, Abraham as an illustration, a warning to the rich, a rebuke of worldliness and what to do when we "face trials of many kinds."[7]

In addition to the Bible itself, there are mature Christians who can help each of us in the application of the Bible's teachings to our daily lives. Such persons must be sought out carefully because there are always those who talk about faith but who lack a personal walk with the Lord. New Christians are advised to have a Christian mentor who can continue to help them to understand the questions and problems they will encounter as new Christians. Those of us who are mature Christians need to be willing to help those who could benefit from our counsel and expressions of faith.

How Does It Relate To Me?

Christians are clearly different from non-Christians. We are set apart by God once we proclaim our steadfast faith. Once we are Christians we will think and act in ways that continue to set us apart. We will put God first in our lives rather than ourselves or others. We will endeavor to keep His Word and obey His commandments. We will ask for forgiveness for our sins. We will worship Him on a regular basis. We will fellowship with other Christians. We will study the Bible. We will live Godly lives following the moral precepts of the Bible. We will seek to lead others to Christ. If these things are more than we are willing to commit to, we have not yet come to understand what it means to be true followers of Christ.

Earlier we talked about what it means to believe intellectually. A person who does this will accept everything that can be proven but will not be willing to "take the leap of faith." Such persons might feel they have met the requirement of John 3:16, but they have not yet come to have a faith. Some people will say they believe but are so self-centered that they cannot let God interfere with their efforts to find pleasure on this earth. Then there are still others who claim to believe but are lazy in following through with their commitment. They might say they are Christians, but they cannot find time to get to church and never seem to have more than a dollar or two to give to the work of the Lord. Such people might be called "couch-potato Christians." Their approach to the rest of life carries over in the lack of any Christian fervor.

What kind of person are you? Did any of the persons described in the previous paragraph sound like you? If so, what will it take to light a fire under you? Are you willing to let others control your life, or are you the one who wants to set personal goals and really wants to have a vibrant Christian faith? God has left the choice with you. What will you do about it?

Knowing God's Will

Have you ever had a friend or co-worker ask you, "What should we do (in this or that particular circumstance)?" and your reaction is that you don't have the slightest clue as to what should be done? Have you ever prayed to God about a situation asking for guidance and then felt that no guidance on that issue ever reached you?

In Matthew 26:39 Jesus prayed to the Father, "...not as I will, but as you will." In Mark 3:35, Jesus speaking to a multitude said, "Whoever does God's will is my brother and sister and mother." In other Scriptures as well, it is clear that there is a will of God and that we should obey that will. Yet, how do we obey God's will when we are unclear as to what that will is.

M. Blaine Smith has written about this issue. His book takes the Christian through the process of "finding guidance for personal decisions."[8] You might find this helpful for additional reading. Smith emphasizes that the issue of finding God's will is a major issue with Christians today. He deals with the important subjects of mistaking a personal desire with God's will, as well as when God takes the initiative as opposed to when we

must do this. And then there is the issue of God's timing—
when God is ready but we might not be ready.

A brief guide to seeking God's will involves the following
steps:

1. **Become a Christian who loves the Lord with all your might.**

   If you are not yet a Christian as you read this, you must
   come humbly to the Lord to accept Him and the gift of
   salvation that He offers you. You cannot communicate
   with a God you have not come to accept. He is waiting
   on you. Whenever you are ready, He is ready too.

2. **Read and study the Bible.**

   You will not really know God until you know His word,
   the Holy Bible. Using a study guide can be very helpful
   whether you are a new or an experienced Christian.
   Studying the Bible in a study group can also be helpful as
   you hear the questions and insights of others. This process will cause you to think about what it means to be a
   Christian. The process must be continuous.

3. **Focus upon an issue which you can clearly define.**

   God's will requires that we know the topic, that we have
   thought this through ourselves to the point of being able
   to describe to God and others in a clear manner just what
   it is that we are praying about. Until we do this, we are
   giving God a situation that is muddled; in fact, we don't
   know what we are talking about. A good way to clarify a
   topic for ourselves is to take a piece of paper and write it
   out. Then read it over. If you are not sure it is clear, ask
   someone else to read it and ask them if they understand it
   without your coaching. It is not that God will not
   understand, the issue is that we must understand what
   we are asking for in order to recognize God's response.

4. Pray earnestly with a clear statement of your request.

Prayer is our language, our method of communicating with God. Through it we let God know our thoughts, our thanks, our requests, and we demonstrate our worship. A time of prayer will be helpful in allowing us to communicate adequately with God. A quick prayer just before we fall asleep or driving down the highway will probably not suffice. Allow God to talk with you during your prayer. Communicating means both talking and listening. Are there some elements of response even during your prayer?

5. Watch and listen.

The story is often told of the man who was told by God that He (God) would come to visit him that day. During the day there were several visitors, each of which needed something from the man. At the end of the day the man prayed to God asking Him why He had not come. God reminded him that He had come in the form of the several visitors. Because the man had treated the visitors well, he proved that he was obedient to God's Word and received God's blessing.

In what form will God come to you?

6. Meditate.

J. I. Packer refers to meditation as "the activity of calling to mind, and thinking over, and dwelling on, and applying to oneself, the various things that one knows about the works and ways and purposes and promises of God."[9] Meditation is introspective in that we are communicating with ourselves. Doing so helps us to clarify who we are (and who we are not), what our goals are, the nature of our obstacles, our strategies and our feelings. It is a thinking process. It is not daydreaming, which is an unorganized series of images and thoughts that are unrelated and without a serious thought process, but it is a time that we think through what God is saying to us. Smith talks about "reasonable circumstantial guidance" that would be a solid guide for the Christian to look for in discovering God's will.

7. Discipline Ourselves.

This means being in control of ourselves in specific ways. R. Kent Hughes suggests that self-discipline must be exercised in our relationships with others in the various roles in which we perform, in our souls including our minds and our prayer and worship, our characters (integrity, our words, our deeds), and ministries (our church activities, our Christian leadership, our giving, our witness).[10] We must discipline ourselves in order to maintain control over our minds and bodies. If we are engaged in sinful behavior, would that affect our ability to hear or see how God is communicating with us?

8. Listen to the Whisper.

Max Lucado, in *When God Whispers Your Name*, relates a number of stories in which God has whispered a message.[11] The magazine *Guideposts* relates story after story in which the evidence suggests the presence and intervention of God. When was the last time God whispered to you?

As A Christian, I Will...

It is time now to consider the action plan each of us will have as Christians. Earlier we had a discussion about setting goals, and this will be covered in greater detail later. Setting goals, however, is not only a good idea, it is also something which is expected of every Christian. As we study the Bible, we come upon many things that we are told to do or to stop doing. Saying Uh-Huh won't do it. We have to be willing to set goals to accomplish that which the Bible commands us to do.

What does the Bible direct you to do? Are you doing all of these things? If not, why is this so?

This book will direct you toward developing personal goals and priorities. You need goals and priorities in regard to your Christian faith as well. Like any goal setting, it begins with where you are now. A good place to begin is to write out what you believe in. Below write a brief description of your faith statement:

My Personal Christian Faith Statement

I believe

You might ask another person to read the statement you wrote. Does this person think that it sounds like you? Rework the statement if necessary. It is important that the statement reflects what you really believe in.

Now in the space below describe the actions you are going to take during the next twelve months concerning your Christian faith:

My Christian Action Plan

Bible Reading/Study

Prayer

Meditation

Other

Do you know what it means to be a Christian? It is essential that you not only understand what it means to be a Christian but also that you have a commitment to act upon that faith. James 2:14 reads, "What good is it, my brothers, if a man claims to have faith but has no deeds?" If you have faith (knowing what it means to be a Christian), you will have the joy and commitment to want to share that faith and to show the love and grace which has been richly bestowed upon you.

Endnotes

[1]J. I. Packer, *Knowing God*, 20th Anniversary Edition (Downers Grove, IL: InterVarsity Press, 1993), pp. 18-19.

[2]Packer, p. 20.

[3]LeRoy Lawson, *Questions For God* (Joplin, MO: College Press Publishing Co.), 1992.

[4]Stephen B. Douglass, *Enjoying Your Walk With God: How To Live Above Your Everyday Circumstances* (San Bernardino, CA: Here's Life Publishers, 1989), pp. 51-66.

[5]Ibid., pp. 91-98.

[6]John L. Morrison, *Alexander Campbell: Educating The Moral Person* (N.P., 1991).

[7]James 1:2.

[8]M. Blaine Smith, *Knowing God's Will: Finding Guidance For Personal Decisions*. Foreword by Richard C. Halverson (Downer's Grove, IL: InterVarsity Press, 1991).

[9]Packer, p. 23.

[10]R. Kent Hughes, *Disciplines Of A Godly Man* (Wheaton, IL: Crossway Books, 1991).

[11]Max Lucado, *When God Whispers Your Name* (Dallas, TX: Word Publishing, 1994).

Chapter Four

Four areas:

Talents, Spiritual Gifts, Education and Abilities

There are different kinds of gifts, but the same Spirit. There are different kinds of service, but the same Lord. There are different kinds of working, but the same God works all of them in all men. Now to each one the manifestation of the Spirit is given for the common good. To one there is given through the Spirit the message of wisdom, to another the message of knowledge by means of the same Spirit, to another faith by the same Spirit, to another gifts of healing by that one Spirit, to another miraculous powers, to another prophecy, to another distinguishing between spirits, to another speaking in different kinds of tongues, and to still another the interpretation of tongues. All these are the work of one and the same Spirit, and he gives them to each one, just as he determines. —
1 Corinthians 12:4-11

It was he who gave some to be apostles, some to be prophets, some to be evangelists, and some to be pastors and teachers, to prepare God's people for works of service, so that the body of Christ may be built up until we all reach unity in the faith and in the knowledge of the Son of God and become mature, attaining to the whole measure of the fullness of Christ. – Ephesians 4:11-13

Hide it under a bushel. No. I'm gonna let it shine. Hide it under a bushel. No. I'm gonna let it shine. Let it shine. Let it shine. Let it shine. – V. O. Fossett[1]

This chapter takes a look at the qualities we as humans possess which allow us to do special things. It is important that all of us become aware of these qualities within ourselves and then devote time and energy to develop these qualities. In addition, we have the opportunity to learn. Most of us have a formal education (school and college) and an informal education (what we learn from others around us). This education adds another dimension to us not only as we develop these qualities (talents, abilities, spiritual gifts), but it also allows us us to develop skills we did not possess before.

These qualities make us become both more capable and more unique as individuals. Because the world requires many unique qualities, this means that we do not have to compete with every other person for each job we apply for or to take advantage of opportunities in society. None of us has developed to the level to which we are capable. You might be fully developed in some areas but not as an overall individual. Thus, potential still exists. There are things you might do in the future which you cannot do now until you develop your talents, abilities and spiritual gifts and acquire more education.

Talents and Abilities

Every Christian has talents and abilities as well as spiritual gifts. Some of us have a formal education as well, but many have done well (have enjoyable lives, contribute to the lives of others) without it. Education becomes a means of building upon the talents, gifts and abilities we have to give us greater opportunities to serve God and others.

Let's return to the common denominator. We all have talents, abilities and spiritual gifts. But you might say, "I don't have any," or "Not many for me." While it is probably true that some people have few talents, gifts or abilities, the Scriptures quoted above from Ephesians 4:11-13 and 1 Corinthians 12:4-11 seem to be adequate proof that God did not create any of us without spiritual gifts. We are assuming as well that none of us is without talents and abilities.

Who Has Talents and Abilities?

This includes you and me. It might take us a while to recognize the talents and abilities we have. Yet upon reflection most of us can, without great difficulty, recall things we have been able to do for God, for others and for ourselves that have glorified God, made life better for others or helped us to achieve a goal. To what extent was that action possible because of a talent, ability or spiritual gift? Refer back to the definitions we gave earlier. You do have talents, abilities and spiritual gifts. No two persons are created the same. We each bring talents and abilities into the world. It is up to us to employ these in service to God and others as well as helping ourselves.

Defining the Terms

Let's pause here to define these terms. What is a **talent**? Webster defines talent as "any natural or special gift or aptitude; eminent ability." What then is an **ability**? What abilities are commonplace and which are special to a smaller portion of the population? Taken together, talents and abilities are similar. A talent might be thought of as a special ability with the outcome of its use evident in various ways to others. The category of abilities includes a host of capacities including attitudes and relationships that are not necessarily special but includes those things which do enrich the lives of others. With these definitions, none can deny that he or she has talents and abilities.

What About Spiritual Gifts?

First Corinthians 7:7 reads, "But each man has his own gift from God, one has this gift, another has that." We assume from this that each person has at least one spiritual gift. Does "each man" refer to Christians only? Probably, but there is some doubt. If it does, then we can say that every Christian has at least one spiritual gift.

But what is a spiritual gift? A spiritual gift refers to a special ability or talent to accomplish something of considerable value to God and to the body of Christ. It is difficult to distinguish between a spiritual gift and just doing something well because of an extra expenditure of effort. In fact, maybe the latter is the reflection of a lesser talent or spiritual gift.

The Bible makes reference to some gifts being more valuable than others in 1 Corinthians 12:28-31. Verse 31 clearly refers to the "best gifts," while verse 28 gives a ranking of spiritual gifts although the list does not include all the spiritual gifts that are mentioned in the New Testament. From this we might conclude that the use of the highest ranking spiritual gifts is extremely important and that having such a gift places a burden on us to be faithful in exercising it regularly and with excellence. "Diversity of tongues" – the gift of interpretation of languages is listed last. What conclusions should we draw from this?

Spiritual gifts are not to be confused with the fruit of the Holy Spirit which are mentioned in Galatians 5. For example, Galatians 5:22-23 states: "But the fruit of the Spirit is love, joy, peace, patience, kindness, goodness, faithfulness, gentleness, and self-control. Against such things there is no law." Spiritual gifts are God-given gifts for His glory in general and for the upbuilding of the church specifically. The fruit of the Spirit are qualities of Christian character for the benefit and blessing of the world in general and, like a sweet perfume, for the church specifically.

Further, spiritual gifts are not rewards for good spiritual conduct or for some other good deed. We do not know on what basis spiritual gifts are given out or denied. In most of us, however, there is reason to believe that we possess more spiritual gifts than we know ourselves. And then there is the additional gap between the spiritual gifts we know we have and those we are willing to admit to or use in the company of others. Might this situation apply to you?

First Peter 4:10 reads, "Each one should use whatever gift he has received to serve others, faithfully administering God's grace in its various forms." To test your "good stewardship," respond to the following question: What is your attitude toward the spiritual gift(s) you have? (Choose one that fits you.)

1. I joyfully use my gift(s) in the praise of the Lord,

2. I am happy to use my gift(s) when others request it,

3. If no one else is available, I am willing to use my gift(s),

4. If asked or given the opportunity, I will pray about it and if the Lord will specifically ask me, I will use my gift(s),

5. I do not want anyone to know I have a spiritual gift and will therefore hide its existence from others, or

6. I will not exercise my spiritual gift(s) (the reasons are my own).

Once you decide whether you will use your spiritual gifts, how do you go about finding your spiritual gifts? The answer rests in what you enjoy doing, what you do well, what others have told you that you do well and the vision you have of what you could become (within the church in the broad sense that is in keeping with His will).

God expects you to utilize your spiritual gift(s) as a good steward. To deny their use is to deny God. God has done so much for you and for me. How can we refuse our God?

Some practical things you might do are:

- Pray for a place to serve.
- Talk to the pastor about what ministries you are interested in.
- Do some study in the areas where you might enjoy serving.

The Impact Of Education

When we think of education we think of school and college. This is where our formal education takes place. In addition, we learn much of what we know, acquire many of the skills we have and develop the perspectives that we carry with us throughout life in places other than school and college. We learn in an informal setting in our churches, our homes, our places of work, with our friends and relatives and with the persons we meet on the street. Informal education is very much a major force within the lives of people today.

Education is really an attitude: an attitude of wanting to learn more, understand deeper, appreciate the viewpoint of another person, develop another skill, structure a perspective of a set of circumstances and people. All of these can be very interesting. Each person who looks at learning as work is consigned to relative ignorance. Learning not only can be fun, it is fun unless you make it drudgery.

Dull people have an attitude which says, "I have learned all that I want to know." Interesting people are constantly learning, observing and asking questions.

Be careful about making the assumption that learning and formal education are the same thing. Some of the most learned people are people with only a fourth grade education. Such persons have continued to learn over a lifetime and have much to share with others about their informal education.

The opportunity to get a formal education is available in democratic countries around the world, and to some extent, in other countries as well. But an opportunity has no value unless you take advantage of it. Although there is no correct amount of formal education, those without a high school diploma find themselves handicapped in the job market. The job opportunities increase as the amount of formal education we have acquired increases. As we move gradually into a much more structured society, this demand for formal education will accelerate. You are encouraged to pursue as much formal education as the goals you have set for yourself in life require. Completing formal education beyond that level will have the capability of enriching your life and your ability to help others.

For Christians the matter of education takes on a special meaning. Whether it be formal education or informal education, we are admonished throughout the Bible to learn about the Scriptures, to learn about God. When we do not engage in Bible study and material related to the Bible, we allow our faith to remain shallow. We can go to heaven without learning very much. Becoming a Christian is quite simple. John 3:16 lays it out for us. But God expects more from us. He expects us to follow the teachings of the Bible as the authoritative guide for our lives. If we don't know the Bible, it surely will not be a major force in our lives.

As you examine your informal and formal education and its impact upon your life, use the following set of questions to help guide you as you encounter the variety of situations life provides for each of us:

1. What is it?

2. How did (does) it happen?

3. Why did (does) it happen?

4. What are the possible impacts?

5. What are the implications for me right now?

6. What opportunities does this set of circumstances provide?

If your typical answer is "I don't care," then no informal or formal education will be able to help you. In fact, nothing much can help you. If your answer is that these are interesting questions, then there is some room for encouragement.

Throughout this book you will notice that you are encouraged to set goals and then determine strategies by which these goals will be reached. If your career goal requires more education—possibly both formal and informal—what are you doing about it? Regardless of your age or your financial capability, what are you doing about it? If you want something strongly enough, you owe it to yourself to act on your need for the education your goals require. When should you act on this? Take the first step within sixty minutes. Take the big step within twenty-four hours. This really is the first day of the rest of your life.

What Should I Do With These Capacities?

How often are you excited about life, about who you are, about what you do, about the people you meet and things you encounter, about the issues which you face? Excited people are interesting people. People who grump their way through life complaining that others do not do enough for them are going to remain dull, uninteresting and have few well-developed friendships.

One of the characteristics of society today and for the next generation is that we are a "learning society." This is related to how easy it is for us to access great amounts of data. If we are to succeed, we are told, it is because we will have access to great amounts of data. Having data is a prerequisite to a learning situation. The more we learn, the more we will realize that we have not mastered a subject. As we come to this realization, we need to adopt an attitude which says, I want to learn as much as I can about a wide variety of things, to come to understand them and their interrelationships and then be able to apply them in the lives of people.

One of the fascinating things about life is that every one of us gets to make the choice of what kind of person he or she will be. Whether you are handicapped, young or old, man or woman, of whatever race or national origin, wherever you live, regardless of the amount of informal or formal education you have, whatever your economic circumstances and whatever your past experiences, **you get to decide who you will be.**

Some skeptics might say, "Sure, I get to be who I want to be." So, I guess I'll be Michael Jordan, Mark Hatfield (former U.S. Senator from Oregon and Christian leader), Billy Graham or Amy Grant. What **does** separate these people from you? Think about it. What is different about them compared to you?

There are some obvious differences. Michael Jordan probably plays basketball better than you do, and Amy Grant probably sings better than you do. Will you ever play basketball as well as Michael Jordan or sing like Amy Grant? The chances are that you won't, but we can't be sure. Maybe you will be a president of a company or a physician. Maybe you will be the person you are right now. Obviously, there are some far-out goals that there is little hope that you can attain. However, if you really did define your personal goals, you have greatly increased your chances of achieving them.

Goals need to be realistic. Rather than to be like Michael Jordan or Amy Grant, your goals might need to be like a person you know in your church or school. Clearly the goals of who we want to be should not be based upon the glory we perceive a Michael Jordan has but **rather upon who we are, what our talents, abilities, spiritual gifts and education compel us to be.** If your goal, based upon your assessment of your talents, abilities, spiritual gifts and education, is to be president of the United States, then work toward that goal. Remember your goal and the strategies you have developed to help you reach that goal. If you change your goals, then change the strategies you are using. But don't relent. Focus on the main thing.

When a football player runs on to the field, he has more than a desire to win, however strong that will might be. In addition, he will know his abilities and talents. He will be in good physical shape. He will know the plays. He will have practiced. He will be focused upon using all of this in the pursuit of winning the game.

Each of us needs to win the game of life. There is a game every day. Some games carry over to the next day or the next week. We won't win every one of them, but we must make the effort to win as many as possible. How many we win will depend heavily upon our physical, spiritual and emotional conditioning, and the preparation we have, including experience and our energized focus, to participate to our fullest capability.

What are your talents, abilities, spiritual gifts and education? What is your focus? What are your goals? What are your strategies?

Endnote

[1]"This Little Light Of Mine," by V. O. Fossett from *Heavenly Highway Hymns* (Nashville, TN: Stamps-Baxter, 1956), 166.

Chapter Five

Understanding Values: What Is Your System?

What Is a System of Values?

A set of values is like a criteria we use to measure whether to buy a car or a refrigerator, to go on a vacation at destination A or B, to go out to eat or eat at home, or whether or not to get up in the morning when the alarm goes off. The values we hold guide us in every important decision we make.

Our value systems tell us whether a decision will be wise or not. There are some decisions we must make which are not guided by our value systems (such as whether to peel the carrots or potatoes first), but our value systems will guide all of our important decisions.

Our value systems are statements about what is important to us. Further, our values even sort out the important things between what is most important compared to what is least important to us.

Being Selfish

We make decisions on the basis of what is important to us. This is not necessarily selfish in itself because worship of God might be our number one priority. Number two might be serving the homeless. Thus, our values are centered upon what is important to us, and they might not be self-serving in the sense that we think of as selfish. Being selfish is serving self to the exclusion of others.

Have you ever been on an airplane and heard the flight attendant announce that in the unlikely event that the passenger cabin should lose air pressure, the tubes and face masks will drop down? Adults, if a child is next to them, are to place the mask on *themselves* first and the child second. Is this being self-centered? Is this saying adults are more important than children (a value statement)? Certainly not.

This procedure exists because this approach could save two lives, the adult and the child. Adults might retain consciousness long enough to put on only one oxygen mask. If they help the child first, after a few moments they might lose consciousness and become unable to save themselves. But with the aid of the air through the mask, the adult can help the child place the mask on safely. The point is that sometimes we have to help ourselves first in order to be able to help others as well as preserve ourselves for further service.

Being selfish is to serve self only or primarily. Benefits are coincidental or accidental. We act as if we do not care about the impact of our actions upon others. We are taught as children not to be selfish.

However, it is OK to have some goals that are selfish. An example might be having your hair done or buying a new outfit because it will make you feel better. The primary goal in such an action is simply that you wanted to do it. The fact is that some portion of our resources (time and money) can fairly be allocated to things that please only ourselves. It could be that others will gain some benefit (such as admiring the new hairdo or new clothes) but that is not the primary goal and, in fact, the action might be taken even if no other person gained from this action.

I am suggesting that it is appropriate for us to have some goals that deal with legitimate personal needs and concerns. If there are things we really want to do, some portion of our time and money should be allocated to fulfilling these desires as long as our primary responsibilities are being met. Each of us is a unique individual and we need to allocate some portion of our time to pursuing that uniqueness as long as it is in keeping with serving God and is consistent with our value systems.

We might argue that there is so much to do in serving others that there isn't time for ourselves. Refer back to the example with the flight attendant. The person on the airplane was better able to help others after first attending to a task related to self. Likewise, if we run ourselves into the ground (exhaust all our resources), we will no longer be in a position to help others.

Each of us needs to think through a plan of how we can be balanced persons both in our thinking and in our relationships with God and others. Part of this strategy requires some time to pursue things that we are interested in either for the moment or on a continuing basis.

Let me give you a personal example. I have a model railroad which takes up one whole room of our house, the room over the garage. I run the railroad, and I build models of railroad cars and buildings simply because this is fun for me. It so happens that my grandchildren get a fair amount of enjoyment from this project, as well as did our children when they were young; but I pursued this hobby even when there were no children or grandchildren in my home. I am pleased that others enjoy my hobby. But, in effect, this is a selfish pursuit which is good for me. The model railroad presents some challenges, but I can limit those challenges to those which I consider fun. The activity draws upon my creativity and is a realization of my fascination with railroads and everything connected with them. I return from my railroad room a better person.

We need to think of how we can make ourselves more effective tools in the service of God and others. This means eating prudently, taking care of our health, sleeping adequately and even pursuing some personal goals and desires. This will have the effect of making each of us a more effective tool in serving God and others. Remember the ax which is used to cut down a tree. While the ax is there for the sole purpose of cutting down the tree, it is much more effective if it is sharpened from time to time.

Balancing Self and Others

After making the case for saying we each should have some selfish values to make us better persons, let's put these particular values into perspective. Maybe our selfish value is hunting or shopping. When should we engage in our personal desires, and when should we be more concerned with serving others? This is the issue of balance.

Excellence in our lives is a matter of balance. Every aspect of our lives has to be seen in relationship to everything else. This brings us back to our values. What is the most important?

In the personal example above, I related that my model railroad is very important to me, but there are many things even more important. If I am engaged in working on my model railroad on a Saturday afternoon and someone in the house or on the phone asks me to do something, what should I do? Unless it is something that can best be done later (like a request to have lunch on Tuesday, something I cannot possibly do on Saturday afternoon), I will normally respond to the matter then as soon as I clean the glue off my fingers or can close down the railroad. Why? Because in my value system, doing things for other people ranks higher than the model railroad, even though both are positive values that I hold.

Is there an activity (physical or in your mind) in your life that needs to be balanced in order to put your values in the correct perspective? There can be a proper time for hunting or shopping, but the attention to that interest might become so great that it conflicts with higher level values such as giving attention to others? The project of writing this book is a high value with me, but it was just interrupted on a Saturday morning to help two granddaughters (ages three and five) find their bathing suits so they could go in the pool with their Oma (grandmother).

We constantly face the issue of balancing what we will do with our resources so that they will coordinate with our values. When too much of our time or money goes to one of our values, it bothers us. This is because we are acting in a manner that is inconsistent with our value systems. Each of us faces a constant struggle for balance every moment of our lives. Thinking about our values constantly will guide us in how we allocate our precious resources and help us to feel good about ourselves and others.

As was discussed earlier in the book, all of us have values. We differ in what values we hold and the behaviors that flow from those values. As long as our values begin with our Christian faith and are always consistent with that faith and biblical values, we can each develop our unique God-given capabilities that enable us to achieve or produce vastly different actions and results. Some of us are good at cleaning the house, others at singing in an opera, while others perform at a computer keyboard. Have the courage to be the person God intended for you to be.

What Is The Relationship Between Faith and Values?

Values are those things we hold dear: the guides for our behavior on a minute-by-minute basis. Our values must include our Christian faith as our first rank in values, our first priority in thought and action.

Not all Christians rank their Christian faith as their number one value. It is possible to believe in God, to accept Jesus as the only risen Savior and to want to follow the Bible but still have other values that we rank higher in our system than this faith.

What are some of the characteristics of having values higher than our Christian faith? Let's look at a few:

- Putting only a dollar or five dollars in the church collection because we argue that we need the rest for our lifestyles.

- Not getting to church on Sunday morning because we are too tired, we are unhappy with something someone at church said or we happen to be traveling that Lord's Day.

- Acting in an unchristian manner in a business deal during the week (this deal might be in the purchase of a toaster).

- Unwillingness to say anything about our faith or church involvement in front of non-Christians because we are concerned that we might be embarrassed.

- Not having a prayer life or not reading the Bible.

The list could be much longer. The items touch upon our time, our thoughts, our money, our actions, our commitments and our relationships with God. Do any of them sound familiar in your life? Should you do something about it? What, specifically, is your plan?

As Christians, our first value should be that we want to be as Christlike as possible based upon our wholehearted acceptance of the Bible and all that it teaches. What are some of the characteristics of Christians who do place their Christian faith as number one in their value systems? Let's look at a few:

- In every action we contemplate, we ask ourselves, "What would Christ do?" And then take that action.

- We give 10% of our financial resources to Christian organizations including our local church.

- We worship with other Christians every Lord's Day regardless of where we are (we avoid conflicts with this time in our scheduling).

- We carefully engage in behavior that will positively reflect upon our Christian faith and our church (we avoid violating the Ten Commandments and follow New Testament teachings about how Christians should behave).

- We engage in prayers each day that direct our thoughts and actions toward God.

- We engage in regular Bible reading.

- We have a ministry in which we are doing the Lord's work in accordance with the talents we possess.

- We are willing and even seek out opportunities to give witness of our Christian faith to others.

- Our Christianity is the center of our lives.

- We are joyous Christians.

Does your Christian faith permeate all that you do, that you have, that you think about and all of your time? If not, then this would be a good time for you to consider what is happening in your Christian faith. Are you serious about your Christian faith? Do you find yourself saying, "I guess I am a Christian." How well did you do on the above list? Maybe a "To Do List" would be appropriate to reflect areas in which your Christian faith is not number one in your value system. We know for sure that **you know where your Christian faith is in your value system. If you need to take action about your Christian faith, have the courage to take it now.**
Whether your faith is number one in your value system or somewhere down the list, here are some Scriptures which you

might want to consult as part of your thinking process relative to your value system.

- "Indeed, the very hairs of your head are all numbered. Don't be afraid; You are worth more than many sparrows" (Luke 12:7). Even God has a value system in which some things are of greater value than others.

- "Therefore, since we have been justified through faith, we have peace with God through our Lord Jesus Christ" (Rom. 5:1). Our faith produces other things which are important in our value systems.

- "...I tell you the truth, if you have faith as small as a mustard seed, you can say to this mountain, Move from here to there; and it will move. Nothing will be impossible for you" (Matt. 17:20). Our faith becomes a vehicle whereby our other lesser values can become a reality if only we believe.

- "For everyone born of God overcomes the world. This is the victory that has overcome the world, even our faith. Who is it that overcomes the world? Only he who believes that Jesus is the Son of God" (1 John 5:4-5). Placing our Christian faith as our number-one value in our personal value systems positions us to achieve victory in all our other values as we overcome the world.

Where Do Our Values Come From?

The answer to this question is not easy. The human mind is the most complex aspect and one of the least understood aspects of life even with all of our research and observation. The Bible gives us some insight but not the whole story. Let's review a few of the things we do know:

- We are all creatures of God—"You are worthy, our Lord and God, to receive glory, and honor and power, for you created all things, and by your will they were created and have their being" (Rev. 4:11) — and have come short of the glory of God — "For all have sinned and fall short of the glory of God" (Rom. 3:23).

- We are created with a will to behave within the parameters of what the human body is capable of doing — "Although they know God's righteous decree that those who do such things deserve death, they not only continue to do these very things but also approve of those who practice them" (Rom. 1:32).

- We are instructed through the Bible and responses to prayer to behave in certain ways — "He has delivered us from such a deadly peril, and he will deliver us. On him we have set our hope that he will continue to deliver us, as you help us by your prayers. Then many will give thanks on our behalf for the gracious favor granted us in answer to the prayers of many" (2 Cor. 1:10-11).

- We are told of the penalties of our sin — "For the wages of sin is death, but the gift of God is eternal life in Christ Jesus our Lord" (Rom. 6:23).

- We are each uniquely different, even at birth.

- We each develop a personality which affects the choices we make.

- We are affected by our experiences which teach us that some things are more desirable than others. A strong experience can have the effect of distorting our perceptions of reality and thus affecting our decisions about our value systems.

- We are all capable of rationalization. We can rationalize that a certain behavior is appropriate because of some factor when this reasoning does not meet the test of logical thinking. We rationalize when we desire a particular outcome and then build a case for that outcome even though it means we select data and observations that are not complete.

• We are most affected by the people around us. We are instructed in the Bible to choose carefully those who are to be around us. "And let us consider how we may spur one another on toward love and good deeds. Let us not give up meeting together, as some are in the habit of doing, but let us encourage one another — and all the more as you see the Day approaching" (Heb. 10:24-25). Our families typically have the greatest influence on us, but as we get older we are often heavily influenced by our experiences with other people. Positive, faithful people will affect us in a positive, faithful way.

• Our value systems begin early. The value system of a child is readily apparent. While not developed in some areas, it is still, nonetheless, there and causes the child to behave in certain ways.

• This value system which we develop early only gradually changes as we get older. Unless we have dramatic experiences, such as being saved, nearly drowning or having a fortieth, fiftieth or sixtieth birthday, the development of our value systems tends to be gradual. Thus, regardless of our age, the value systems we now have began when we were children and have gradually gone through refinements as we have aged.

• While this cannot be proven, I suspect that we tend to change only small parts of our value systems (except for that dramatic experience) because most of our experiences in life are not all encompassing. That is, most experiences are rather specific. We tend to generalize from these experiences, however, to form general principles which become part of our value systems. When a general principle is formed, it is tested automatically against our value systems. We then decide to accept (change our value systems) or reject the newly developed generalization. We often do this without realizing that the experience we just had will have the effect of changing our value systems forever.

- Our value systems change in imperceptible ways every day. Each of us views the world differently today than we did yesterday. It is hard for any of us to see the difference from day-to-day unless the change has been dramatic. But we should not confuse mood changes with permanent changes in our value systems. Any change in our value systems will affect our values from that time forward. A mood will come and go and probably return.

- Each of us is in control of the development of our value systems.

- How can we ensure that the development of our value systems is gradually making us better persons? Some suggestions are:

  1. Remain close to God.

  2. Remain in the fellowship of fellow believers.

  3. Read the Bible regularly.

  4. Pray constantly.

  5. Avoid things that draw us from the positive (people who draw us toward negative experiences, certain television programs, certain reading materials, certain places where we will not have positive, uplifting experiences).

  6. Have personal and spiritual goals along with strategies for accomplishing them.

7. Use your mind. Think about who you are and what you want to do with your life. Then have the courage to do it if it falls within God's will for your life.

Where do our values come from? They come from a myriad of sources over a lifetime. They come from positive sources as well as negative sources. They come from the development of our personalities. Our early values, largely taught by parents, become the basis of complex value systems we will develop over a lifetime.

My own parents, Adrian J. (J. doesn't represent a name) and Marguerite Florence Oosting, are now ninety-six and ninety-four and continue to do well. They live in their own home in North Muskegon, Michigan, and Dad drives the car on most days as they go to the market or just go for a ride. Both of them are strong Christians and they come from strong Christian lineage (Dad is 100 percent Dutch and Mother is 50 percent Dutch and 50 percent German). They have attended the Reformed Church throughout their lives while Dad was an insurance agent until he retired at age seventy-nine. They instilled a strong Christian faith in me as a youngster and many of my early, fond memories relate to the church and the other factors leading to the early development of my faith as the foundation of my value system.

Although my parents met in college reflecting the importance of education in their value systems, I decided to make getting a formal education an even higher priority in my value system. Encouraged by my parents and then by my wife, Jackie, I became the only child of my parents to obtain a college degree. Later, I went on for the Ph.D. This became a part of my value system. It was not the same value system that my parents had, but it was consistent with theirs. While they did not seek graduate degrees themselves, they encouraged me to obtain one. Thus, Christians with different but consistent value systems can encourage each other to achieve goals that they themselves do not have as their own goals.

In the development of our value systems, we need to be close to the will of God and this is best determined by:

- Prayer

- Bible study

- Christian fellowship with fellow believers.

When Do We Learn Our Values?

The section above provides some of the answers to this question as it addresses the issue of the source of our value systems. We learn from a variety of sources as we are in contact with them. Even though most of the influence from my parents came before I was twenty, they are still a guiding light in my value system. Now my wife has become the principal force in the development of my value system, and my children and grandchildren are having an influence as well.

Our value systems develop gradually so we continue to learn and be affected by our experiences and observations throughout our lives. While our value systems do not change rapidly unless we have a life-changing experience or observation, they do continue to change. For some of us that rate of change is more rapid and for some it changes so much that it leaves our lives in a state of some turmoil. It is comforting for us to have a set of values that does not need to change. Such a pillar comes from our Christian faith.

People who are not Christians also have value systems but they lack this pillar of Christian faith. Their value systems might be based upon many of the same principles (such as from the Ten Commandments), but without the guiding faith that goes with the Christian faith. These are often seen as good, law-abiding people who do not accept Christianity as a central part of their value systems.

Those who have neither faith nor a set of steadfast principles by which to guide their lives are more at sea in the quest for meaning and satisfaction in life than Christians are. They lack value systems which provide positive encouragement and rewards. Although they might have some of the values Christians also hold, which values they hold could be haphazard.

It is said that there is a code of honor even among thieves—some things that even the lowest thief or other criminal looks down upon.

All of us continue to adjust our values (which ones are important to us and how they rank among the total set of values we hold). Those of us who are constantly wanting to learn and engage in behavior like reading and asking questions are more likely to be open to changes in our value systems. Our top ten values will not change much, but as we work our way through life, some of the lower level values are bound to change. At age seventeen we might enjoy playing football or being cheerleaders while at age thirty both of these might be relegated to good memories rather than current values we hold for our lives today.

Because we adjust our values as we go through life, it is essential that we are able to tell the difference between principles and preferences. Principles are elements such as our Christian faith, our ethical operating systems, our life goals. Preferences are such elements as wanting to go somewhere in the morning rather than the afternoon because of personal convenience. The concept of principle vs. preference will be discussed more completely in another part of this book.

Why Are Some People More Values (Principles) Driven Than Others?

Each human being is different. We each differ in several areas. They are:

- our value systems,
- our experiences,
- our talents and spiritual gifts,
- our energy,
- our motivation,
- our personalities and
- our goals.

Our Backgrounds

We might look at three of these areas—our value systems, our experiences and our talents and spiritual gifts—as our backgrounds. Two people who are very similar in these three areas might turn out to be quite different from one another. It is true that some elements in our value systems (hard work being essential, for example), some experiences (such as success in completing a difficult task affecting our motivation) and some parts of our spiritual gifts and talents (the ability to make difficult things simple, for example) might be more than background. They might propel us onward to other activities. However, we could look at these things as affecting our motivation.

These three background items might be seen as the core which makes each of us unique persons. These are the backbone, the essence. They are essential in determining what we are capable of becoming. While some of them (such as our experiences and to some extent our values) can be affected (changed), they are not easily changed to the extent that we become different persons.

Look at yourself and possibly another person you know well. Analyze yourself and this person (do this separately to avoid mixing characteristics) in terms of value systems (including faith), experiences, talents and spiritual gifts. Are there essential gaps in your understanding of the basic elements, the background of the other person or yourself? The remaining characteristics are still to be added, but these form the core of who we are.

Our Action Characteristics

Our action characteristics, then, are the remaining ones listed above. They include:

- our energy,
- our motivation,

- our personalities and
- our goals.

Energy

Most books give little attention to personal energy. I believe it makes up much of the difference in human beings. The condition of our health determines our energy, but even very healthy persons differ considerably in the amount of energy they possess. Why this is true is left for other volumes to explore. Good health and energy are not the same. The point here is that they are different.

It would be easy to confuse energy and motivation. What is the effect of one person having much more energy than other people? Energy does not necessarily reflect motivation. Each of us has seen examples of people who have lots of energy, yet they go in many directions at the same time in using up this energy. Watch a typical two-year-old. When they are awake, they tend to have a lot of energy. Their attention span for any one activity is short. They respond to their emotions, to their interests (toys, parents, etc.) and to stimuli that happens to be visible to them. Their energy has little to do with motivation. As children get older, a five-year-old, for example, the correlation between energy and motivation becomes stronger. They begin to be motivated toward certain behaviors and begin to channel their energy into these behaviors. Their coordination is still clumsy at times, but they are beginning to put the two together.

Some adults are like the two-year-olds. They do not understand how to correlate their energy with their motivation. While they are motivated toward certain behaviors, their energy is used in other ways. As mature adults we must learn how to harness our energy. Just as we can harness the power in electrical energy by creating it and then channeling it into a system that we can use at any outlet in our homes, so must we utilize all the energy we have toward the behaviors that are productive and that help to accomplish our goals.

Motivation

Motivation compels us to act. All of us have some motivation to eat, sleep and breathe. Most of us go beyond this to complete actions that will bring satisfaction to ourselves. The next stage would be to accomplish goals which bring satisfaction to others. Beyond that is the motivation to make life on earth more enjoyable for many others over a long period of time.

What motivates us? Our values form an essential part of the answer. We are motivated to do that which our values tell us we should be motivated to do. For example, Christians are motivated to live Godly lives and to tell others about Jesus. This comes from our commitment to be Christians — we are convinced that to be a Christian means that we must do these things. To avoid doing these things would put our standing as Christians in question. Thus we are motivated to act in certain ways because our values tell us that we must engage in certain behaviors.

Because God is always the same — "Jesus Christ is the same yesterday and today and forever" (Heb. 13:8), why then aren't all Christians the same? Part of the answer is that our talents and spiritual gifts are not the same. Further, we do not all have the same amount of energy, intelligence, opportunity, self-confidence, education or good health. All of these factors tend to make each of us unique. A particular combination of these factors will produce a John Wesley, a Martin Luther or a Billy Graham. Equally important are the many saints who are not as well known who have been motivated to great heights in service to God and man. Each of us can probably think of some people we have known who fit this description.

Maybe even this doesn't adequately describe what motivates us. Motivation is not fully understood. An examination of the literature about motivation will help us understand the various theories of motivation, but none will give us a full understanding of motivation. We do know that some Christians are more motivated than others. These highly motivated Christians have an impact upon society and Christianity. It is hoped that the message of this book will help many people to increase their motivation to set goals, to try to accomplish those goals and even to succeed in many areas.

Personality

We begin to develop our unique personalities early in life. The personality of the Christian is developed around his or her Christian faith and is consistent with it. We express ourselves through our personalities. We tend to characterize our personalities by such terms as "outgoing," "introvert," "talkative," "nice person," "likable," "jerk," "self-centered," "nerd" and "friendly."

When interviewing people for positions I like to ask them to describe their personalities. What I am looking for is not so much accuracy but the ability of these persons to come to grasp with who they are and how they feel about the personality they describe. If we have a healthy self-concept, we are likely to describe ourselves in positive and fairly accurate terms.

How would you describe your personality? What personality characteristics do you have that are positive? Do you have some negative characteristics? Are all personality characteristics negative or positive? Some of the characteristics we might describe become really positive or negative depending upon the extent to which they are developed within us. For example, if your whole personality is described as "likable" it might mean that you are so intense about being likable that you avoid taking a stand in order not to be seen as "unlikable" to others. The best personality is a balanced personality which reflects a positive set of Christian values and a healthy self-concept.

Goals

Some individuals are more organized than others. The more organized person is likely to have written goals. Do you have written goals? If so, are they for today, this month, this year or the rest of your life?

All of us have some goals. Most of us, however, do not write them down beyond a grocery list of things we intend to buy at the store. Nonetheless, our behavior is guided by these goals.

Why do people have goals? Most of us have incorporated a sense of progress into our value systems. In whatever we do, we feel that we must make progress. It might be pulling weeds in the flower garden or it might be checking off things on our "to-do list" at work. We tend to feel a need to get something done. Some of us are even compulsive about this need to the point of becoming miserable because we can never get enough things done. We even sacrifice quality in order to get a greater number of things "done."

It is healthy to have goals. It gives direction and a sense of purpose and meaning to our lives. Those of us with written goals have the added advantage of feeling that our goals are under control because we have identified them and have spelled them out on a piece of paper. We tend to have the nagging feeling, however, that there are other goals we did not think of at the time we prepared our lists. Even those without written goals have the opportunity to think about goals and have them in their minds as they organize their days. Those who have little sense of what their goals are or who look to others for their goals each day are also likely to have little sense of purpose or the satisfaction that their lives have meaning.

We tend to accomplish more by setting goals. We usually accomplish even more when those goals are firmly fixed in our minds. If we have more than two or three goals, they will not be clear in our minds unless they are written down and kept in a place where we can readily and continually refer to them. More is said about goals in other parts of this book.

We began this section by asking the question, "Why are some people more values (principles) driven than others?" We do know that some people are more likely to act on their values than others. We hope that the above discussion has been helpful even if it is incomplete in its exploration of why some of us are more action oriented than others and why some of us feel compelled to act out our values to the fullest possible extent.

The greatest advantage to this discussion could be in getting each of us to think about these factors as they relate to us each day. To what extent do you act upon your values? Are you comfortable about your answer? If not, what are you going to do about it?

You possibly don't see the distinction drawn here between background and action characteristics. This is not essential to your understanding of yourself or others. In this case, look at the seven characteristics as a whole to understand both yourself and others. These characteristics are provided to give you handles on the individual qualities of human beings and to help you understand yourself. The important thing is to understand as much as the human mind is capable of understanding (beyond understanding is faith).

What Is My Value System?

So far we have talked about value systems and established that you have one. Now would be a good time to look at what your value system includes and in what priority?

How do you identify your value system? It requires looking at goals, interests, past behavior, memberships, your checkbook and your appointment book. There might be some other indicators of how you have spent your assets of time and money as well as certain patterns of behavior. If these exist for you, examine them.

Perhaps the best way to identify (discover) your own value system is to look at past behavior. How have you spent your resources, your time and your money? What have been your thoughts? Who are your friends? What do you feel good about when it happens? What do you like to avoid? Everything we do or refrain from doing reveals much about ourselves. The real us is in our value systems.

In other sections of this book you will have the opportunity to examine your own value system. Each of us has a value system. But what is it? It is important to know as much as you can about your value system and to have your behavior match your value system (thus keeping your conscience clear).

In times of stress we have less opportunity to shield ourselves from others. We become more "transparent" in the sense of the explanations of Grant Howard in his book, *The Trauma of Transparency*.[1] Howard presents the idea that each of us has shields that keep us from being transparent to others. Yet we enjoy life more and are more likely to achieve our goals when we allow ourselves to become more transparent to others.

Is It Possible To Have a "Bad" Set of Values?

"Bad" suggests measurement against some standard. What standards might exist for determining whether your value system is "bad"? One standard is the Bible and what it says about the values a Christian should hold. Another is what society says about our values and the actions that follow from them. Another is the approval or disapproval of our friends. Let's look at these three.

- *The Bible:* A "bad set of values" can only be defined by the extent to which our values are matched up with what the Bible teaches and what society says about our values (and resulting behavior). These two are often very different but it does depend upon the area of activity. The Bible and society differ considerably about what is moral and just. The two sources are much closer together in viewing the beauty of a flower. Thus it is possible to be seen as having a "bad" set of values from the view of Christianity while society either looks the other way (is complacent) or is disdainful about certain values and resulting behavior (such as street corner preaching).

   Society will put pressure upon each of us not to be very strong in our faith and not to be very active. We might be called "religious nuts" or "zealots." However, it is essential for each of us to discover our positive values and then live them out regardless of how they are looked down upon by society.

The Bible is very explicit about certain values: "You shall have no other gods before me" (Ex. 20:3); see also "Do not worship any other god, for the Lord, whose name is jealous is a jealous God" (Ex. 34:14). On the other hand, the Bible is silent on other matters (whom to marry, what career to enter). We can follow the Bible where the Bible speaks; but when it is silent, we must determine our values by their consistency with other Christian values. Ultimately, when the Bible is silent we must ask the question, "How would Christ address this situation?"[2]

When the Bible speaks and we disobey, we have a "bad" set of values. We must conform to the Bible as we understand it after a serious period of Bible study and prayer.

- *Society:* It is possible that society will have laws about our particular behavior that impose a penalty (jail or fine) when we persist in behavior that is not considered safe, appropriate and even comfortable to others. Here we must come back to the issue of principle vs. preference. Is our behavior based upon a principle or a preference? We must stand up for our principles while at the same time be willing to engage in negotiations concerning our preferences. We might be willing to go to jail to defend a principle; but seldom, if we are thinking, for a preference. Some of our values are related to principles, others are related to preferences. I prefer blue over other colors in most situations, but this value is not a principle on which I stand regardless of the circumstances. The wise person can readily differentiate between personal values and preferences and behaves in different ways involving principles as opposed to preferences.

Society, as indicated several paragraphs above, also exerts subtle or direct pressure upon us to behave in certain ways. Societal pressure might seek to convince us that our principles, or values, are "bad values" because they do not conform to the prevailing values of society at the time. Society's success in influencing us will depend upon three variables: (1) the strength of society's values and the willingness of society leaders to push those values, (2) our extent of contact with and dependence upon society and (3) our strength in holding to our principles (values) when they differ from those of others, including those of society as a whole.

- *Friends:* Since our friends are a subset of society, many of the same issues are relevant here. Our friends are the people we trust and the people upon whom we depend for many things including our sense of belonging and worthiness. Because we hold our friends in high regard, we are often willing to do something because our friends have suggested it or have done it themselves with apparent positive results. If our friends have values that society as a whole considers "bad values," then we are likely to share these "bad values" because we are not going to act in ways that are contrary to the values of our friends. Doing so puts the Christian in a bind. Our faith teaches one set of values while our friends advocate a different and contrasting set of values.

  One of the lessons here for Christians is to seek friends who share their values. Although you can evangelize the non-Christian, he or she is not your long-term friend. Your friends are those who strengthen and nurture you in your faith, your value system. To do so they must share this faith, and consequently your value system.

  Thus, it is possible to have a "bad set of values," as witnessed by people who are in trouble with the law including those who are in prison. Their values and corresponding behavior were considered unacceptable by society. As a result, they are isolated from society to avoid any additional negative effects from their behavior.

Why Does It Matter About Our Values?

Why does anything matter? Our values separate us from wild animals. Animals do not understand the difference between what is right and what is wrong. Human beings usually do distinguish that difference once they are past childhood. When we know what is right, our consciences compel us to do what is right. Our consciences are guided by our values. As long as we meet the test above about having values that are in line with the teachings of the Bible, we are pretty safe in following our consciences in making the choices in life. In the examples below read about the situations these persons faced. What values did they hold and what choices did they have to make?

Applying Our Values #1

Marvin VandenBerg would describe himself as a person who liked to be independent and creative. He might add ambitious, having a desire to make money, fiscally responsible, outgoing, not afraid of doing something different and wanting to be able to contribute something to society. He had worked for a medium-sized company in the city where he grew up for the past nineteen years in a middle management position. He and his wife Sally had saved up $23,000 during their eighteen years of marriage, although now they faced the possibility of one of their children wanting to go away to college in another year.

Marvin was becoming more restless about his future. Together Sally and Marvin came up with the idea of going to a bed-and-breakfast for the weekend about 150 miles from home with the children staying at home. In this setting they considered their situation. On the way there they were both rather quiet, but Marvin had a number of ideas flitting through his mind.

On Friday night they made up a list of things they needed to talk about. One was to discuss why Marvin should stay in his current job while another dealt with what possibilities existed for change. What would the impact be on the family v.... change? What did Marvin want to accomplish? What would the cost of independence be? In what way would Marvin do business? What values would guide a new business—making a profit, providing a service to customers, being ethical, following laws and government regulations, knowledge of the product, vendor relations and working with customers? What specific business should Marvin enter? What level of risk would Marvin and Sally be comfortable with handling? Should he stay where he is?

On Saturday they discussed these matters. They decided on a franchise business in a nearby location that served people in a retail relationship. They agreed on a statement of ethics that would guide their relationships with others.

On Sunday morning they attended a church service before returning home. The Scripture passage for the sermon came from 1 Corinthians 11:28-32:

> A man ought to examine himself before he eats of the bread and drinks of the cup. For anyone who eats and drinks without recognizing the body of the Lord eats and drinks judgment on himself. That is why many among you are weak and sick, and a number of you have fallen asleep. But if we judged ourselves, we would not come under judgment. When we are judged by the Lord, we are being disciplined so that we will not be condemned with the world.

The minister's first point was that man should examine himself and do so in concert with God. The second point was that each of us is reluctant to judge or evaluate himself or herself. The third point was that we must be open to being chastened by the Lord.

Marvin thought about these points. First of all, he reasoned, this weekend is my self-examination. I prayed to God for guidance so I must be doing it in concert with God. The second point, however, troubled him. Was he fairly evaluating his own ability to go into business for himself? Did he have a real handle on what he did well and what his shortcomings might be? What if he were wrong? On the third point, he wondered if the Lord would chasten him or tell him to avoid going into this business. After a personal prayer, Marvin was convinced that if the Lord spoke to him about this business he was considering, he (Marvin) would certainly take heed.

On the way home that day Marvin and Sally talked about how God's will is made known in their lives. Marvin thought about an illustration used by their Sunday School teacher. It seems there was a fellow who was in an area that was flooding. A boat came along but the man turned down a ride on the basis that God would save him. As the waters came higher, he turned down a second boat on the same basis. Finally a helicopter came by to get him; but, as he stood on his roof, he declined, saying that God would save him. When he got to heaven he was angry and asked God why He had not saved him. God replied, "But I sent two boats and a helicopter."

Marvin thought about this and concluded there were at least two points to draw from this illustration. One was that we don't always recognize God's intervention in our lives. The second was that responding to God required some active response on the part of the man. He expected God to pluck him off the roof. He did not accept the fact that he had to be willing to climb into the boat or helicopter. Marvin, in thinking about this, asked himself, when have I seen God today? He concluded that the best things on earth happen when God and one or more humans work together to bring a plan into action.

In the following weeks Marvin and Sally explored the possibilities of making their plan work. The children had adequate opportunity to contribute ideas. Doors kept opening to the concept. The concept gradually became more than an idea as they developed specific plans, financial arrangements, timing and an offer by the present employer to let him go with a severance package. Still, Marvin thought, is this the right thing to do? Is this God's will? Do I have the courage to take this step?

Marvin and Sally took the step. There were rough edges, particularly where their lack of experience had blinded them to some of the issues they would face. But they stumbled through these and the business opened. They were pleased although Marvin remained worried about whether he had done the right thing.

One morning Marvin was reading the paper and noticed that one of his principal competitors had a fire the night before which meant he would be out of business for some time. Marvin first reacted with great excitement. He would have less competition and would, thus, more likely be successful. He was running a small profit on a small margin so an increase in business would help to change things for the better.

Then Marvin thought, what if that fire had happened to me? Who would help me? Anyone? Would God send a helicopter? Without saying anything to anyone in the store except that he would be gone for an hour or two, Marvin got into his car. Before starting the engine, he prayed for the right thing to do. He drove to the store that had burned out the night before. He saw the owner whom he had only met one time before briefly and then under circumstances not completely pleasant because this man had not welcomed Marvin as another competitor. When he saw Marvin, he tried to avoid him because he thought that he had come to try to take advantage of him when he was down by offering to buy what was left of the business for a few dollars. Marvin instead went and just stood by the man as he looked through the rubble and found an item here and there worth saving. Marvin told the man he was sorry about what had happened. Marvin asked what he could do to help. The man told him to mind his own business. Marvin then said that this could have just as well happened to him and that he wanted to find some way to help him. The man turned to look at him to try to determine whether to believe him. Marvin was sincere.

The two men went for a cup of coffee. During that time they figured out that the greatest need was to service current customers and provide storage for the items that were only slightly damaged or not damaged at all. Marvin offered to store those items without cost in a part of his building that he had for later expansion and to let the man use these facilities in the interim to service his own customers. Marvin spent the rest of the day working with the man to put the plan into effect. The next day the man had a trailer with generator power in front of the burned-out building with a sign that he was in business.

Marvin was not sure how to explain his day to Sally that evening. She knew about the fire but not what Marvin had done. He did not know whether he had done something foolish or something good. She looked at him strangely as he explained the scenario. She asked him why he had done this. Marvin was not sure. He sought out a quiet corner to meditate with God. He needed to think this through.

The next day two more events took place. In one case a customer came in very angry about the quality of work done by one of Marvin's employees. Marvin felt the employee had probably handled the situation properly and that the customer was unreasonable. Nevertheless, he refunded the payment and the customer, still angry, left.

The second event came when an employee with considerable talent which was not being used came to Marvin and quit claiming that Marvin was unethical in a situation in which Marvin was considering switching to a different vendor for a major source of raw materials. The employee argued that they had a contract with the first vendor and that even considering working with another vendor was unethical. Marvin tried to reason that the first vendor was not meeting their needs and that he would not break the contract unless that vendor agreed. He was considering another vendor as a backup in case he could not resolve the matter with the first vendor. Nevertheless, the employee said "I quit" and walked out cursing Marvin and again saying he was unethical.

Marvin was disturbed by this chain of events. Was he just a pushover who could not succeed in business? Was he really unethical? Did he know how to satisfy customers? Did he really understand what he was doing by going into business for himself?

There was a deeper issue than his competence or whether he was a pushover. Marvin's main concern was whether he was in fact ethical in how he was conducting his business.

Applying Our Values #2

Arthur and Melissa were married while they were both in college. They lived frugally in a married students' apartment to allow themselves to continue with college while holding down part-time jobs. They received some financial support from both sets of parents to meet their expenses during this period. Both were Christians and had waited until marriage to have their first sexual experience. Within a year after graduation the first child came.

They both received job offers in the same vicinity that were based upon their degrees, and they happily accepted. They rented a small house and bought a better car. A second child had come by the time of their fifth anniversary. By the time of their seventh wedding anniversary they were able to buy a house. Their careers were going fine, and they were evidently in love with one another.

Tragedy struck soon after they reached ten years out of college. They were in an auto accident in which they were hit by another vehicle and Arthur was killed. Melissa continued in her job and cared for the two children. She was lonely and missed Arthur. Then one day a year or so later a man she had known for some time asked her for a date. He had never married and had been waiting for the right person to come along. He was a Christian as well, and they started going to church and other activities together. After getting to know one another, they began to talk about marriage. Later on he proposed, and they announced to their friends that they would be married in the spring. One evening when they were together after a romantic dinner in their favorite restaurant, he began to make sexual advances.

Melissa had to make a choice. Her values told her that sexual intercourse was reserved for married couples. Yet they both had sexual yearnings, and they were planning to get married. After all, they were both adults. In television programs and with some of their friends, sex outside of marriage was the norm. If she did not accept his advances, she might lose this opportunity to be married and happy once again. What should she do?

After reading the two brief case studies, we can ask the question again. Why does it matter about our values? Each of us must live with the relationship between our values and our behavior. When the two of them are consistently together, we can be at peace with ourselves. When we, either consistently or in a single situation that we consider important, behave in a manner that is inconsistent with our values, what are the consequences we might pay? We could list some of them here. However, possibly the best answer to this question comes from your own personal lives. When have you consistently behaved in a manner that you knew was not in keeping with your values? How about being on a diet that had its origin in your values and then hiding away a box of cookies or chocolate cake? Or, in the case of Melissa above, when have you engaged in a single behavior that was inconsistent with your values? Perhaps they were not as major as Melissa's, but possibly you said something unkind and rationalized it by thinking that under the circumstances it would be okay. This could have been a minor event or it might have been a major one. Either way we have the problem of a conscience guided by our values and one or more behaviors on our part that are inconsistent with that conscience.

We cannot change our pasts. For the most part, we cannot even change how other people think about our pasts. We can change our presents and our futures. If your current behavior (or plan for the future) is inconsistent with your value system that is itself consistent with the teachings of the Bible, you can do something about it right now. Just one more indulgence is not addressing the problem. One more indulgence is making the problem worse.

As mentioned elsewhere in this book, you are encouraged to **take control of your life.** Rather than letting your life be guided by others or by the indulgences of the moment, think of your values, of what is best for you in the long run. Take care of your health. Take care of your relationships with others. Deepen your faith at every opportunity. The person who is consumed with the positive aspects of life has little time for the things of life that lead us astray. Be active in your church. Find other

people who need your help, and devote yourself to m
lives more enjoyable. The underlying considera
summed up as follows:

- Be a Christian for all that this means. Have faith in God,
  read your Bible and pray. Provide a Christian witness to
  others.

- Develop a value system that starts with your Christian
  faith and is then consistent with the teachings of the Bible.
  Start with the Ten Commandments. Read your Bible, particularly the New Testament, to find the commands of God
  for your daily life. Build them into your value system.

- Live a life that is consistent with this value system. Every
  day in every circumstance. When you have followed the
  two steps above, your conscience will guide you in what
  is right and wrong. Always, not usually, do what is right.
  Your reward will be a life that is at peace with God and at
  peace with yourself. Further, you will be a witness to others about what a godly life can be.

Can We Change Our Values?

Our values will gradually change over our lifetimes. This is
particularly true in the **things** we value. As children we valued
certain things that might become unimportant to us as adults.
As adults we value certain things throughout our lives, and we
lose interest in some things while gaining interest in others.

Our values relating to our faith will change as well. As we
mature as Christians, we develop more consistent values as we
discover more thoughts and behaviors that we are commanded
to have and do. Reading the Bible and praying will help us
develop as Christians. Fellowship with other Christians will
help us develop as Christians. You have heard the term "mature Christian." This describes the person who has devoted the
time and energy to develop his or her Christian faith in study,
prayer and in application with others. These are the persons

we look up to when we need guidance. They are the ones who can provide support to those in need. This should be the goal of each of us. Because our talents and our spiritual gifts differ, each "mature Christian" will be a little different. We need to explore our talents and spiritual gifts to become the Christians God intended us to be. Doing so involves adjusting our values toward becoming the persons God would have us become.

Our values relating to our work situations and our families will gradually change as well. Part of this is related to our emotional maturity. As we become more mature emotionally, we develop strengths and we develop greater insights into life. These will bring about subtle changes in our value systems. As long as we are acting in a manner that is consistent with the Bible and we are at peace with God, we should not resist these changes. These are refinements to our value systems that make us more capable, more able to serve God and others. These strengths can be used to our advantage and those around us as long as they are used consistently with our Bible-based value systems.

Our increased insight into life can help us to discover new ways to serve God and others. We will surely have opportunities to serve. The major limitation for many of us is our ability to get outside of ourselves to see the opportunities before us. God will use us if we develop our talents and spiritual gifts and are willing to be deployed in His service. The more we focus on the world outside of ourselves, the greater becomes the opportunity to serve God through serving others. While there are rewards that often (but not in every circumstance) come from serving others (such as appreciation), the greatest reward is knowing that we are serving our God and that we are living in a manner that is consistent with our value systems.

Endnotes

[1]Grant Howard, *The Trauma Of Transparency: A Biblical Approach To Interpersonal Communication,* Second Edition (Franklin, TN: JKO Publishing, 1997).

[2]"To this you were called, because Christ suffered for you, leaving you an example, that you should follow in his steps" (1 Peter 2:21).

Chapter Six

Setting Goals: What Do You Want To Happen?

Already Existing Goals: Are They Consistent With Our Value Systems?

In the last chapter we dealt with the issue of values including how each of us has a value system. Almost everyone also has goals. Some people set priorities among their goals, and a few develop well-thought-out strategies for accomplishing the goals.

Even before we set any goals, we already have value systems. Are the goals we set always consistent with our value systems? The answer is no. "Why is that?" you might ask.

Most of the time our goals are consistent with our value systems. People, however, sometimes set goals that are inconsistent with their value systems when they are only semiconscious of their values and only slightly more conscious of the goals they set.

To illustrate this point, I suggest that you take out a piece of paper and write down all the values that you have. Even if you spend days compiling the list it will be incomplete, and you won't be satisfied that you have adequately and clearly expressed the values which are recorded. Why is that? It is difficult for any of us to describe ourselves adequately. We can easily hit upon a few of our characteristics and values, but we find it difficult to describe ourselves very well to others.

Values are such an integral part of our inner selves that it is difficult to describe that aspect of ourselves accurately. We take our values for granted. They are like a system against which we can measure any proposed action and get an immediate response. If there is a guilty feeling about a particular act, we immediately know that the act runs counter to our value systems. If we feel good about a series of actions and experience no pangs of remorse, it is likely something that is consistent with our value systems.

We can test any action against our value systems by thinking it through as well. We might consider telling a lie or committing adultery. We can ask ourselves what our value systems would say about those things. If our answer is no (we cannot do those things), then we know that to do so means running against our value systems. If our answer is yes, then we have value systems that will permit such things.

Over a long period of time, **our behavior will be consistent with our value systems.** Our values drive our behavior. At times we act inconsistently; but in most situations and over a period of time, we do, in fact, act consistently with our values.

Why do we sometimes act inconsistently? First, there are times when we act on impulse, without thinking about what we are doing. We end up questioning ourselves, "Why did I do that?" Second, there are inconsistencies within our value systems. We enjoy cookies and looking trim at the same time. Sometimes cookies win out. Third, there are times when we behave according to what we think will win us approval from others or when we act out of a fear of being different. An example of this is the person who drinks alcohol at a party because it appears that everyone else is drinking alcohol and there might be social pressure if he or she were the only one to refuse the drinks. The thinking (not impulsive) person who acts on the basis of principles (values) seldom has the problem of behavior that is inconsistent with his or her values. This person is typically an individual with either a strong conviction about his or her values or a strong personality or both.

Writing a Personal Vision Statement

As I am writing this I can look up and see the waves break on the beach of the Atlantic Ocean. A part of my vision statement is to enjoy some of the beauty of this world and to do so when possible in a style that is marked by excellence but not opulence and that is fiscally responsible. Staying in this hotel with my wife for several days to make progress in the writing of this book has been a good investment in my time (my second most precious resource) and my mind (my most precious resource).

What makes up your vision? How do you go about writing a vision statement? Remember that a vision statement does not need to be succinct. What it does need to do is include as many of the things that you hope for while realizing that, even with the greatest of effort, some of them will not come to pass. A vision statement for a fifty-year-old man or woman who has never played tennis before will not include being able to play tennis like any of the current tennis stars. This goes beyond a desire. A vision is not a fantasy. This will have to be left to daydreams. A vision should include those things that are just maybe attainable if everything in the world were to fall into place in an ideal way.

Now we all have fantasies. I love to play baseball although I seldom have the opportunity. As a young man I thought I would like to be able to play baseball the way my baseball hero played. This was Al Kaline of the Detroit Tigers. He played right field and won the American League batting championship. I was able to play quite well, even playing softball in a church league at the age of fifty-two, but I never compared very closely to Al Kaline as a baseball player. To do so was my fantasy. What are your fantasies?

A vision would be closer to the "dreams" of Rev. Martin Luther King. When he said "I have a dream..." he spoke of a world that most of us recognized as being a world toward which we would like to work. His eloquent words spoke of a world that we knew would not be completely attainable, but we knew that with working together many of the goals could come to pass. Today some of his dream has become a reality and more is yet to come. We are encouraged by the occasional statesman like Dr. King who can project the dreams of our society. We need more leaders in our world who have a dream and are willing to share it with us.

I have some dreams that are coming true. You probably do as well. You also probably have some that you put on the shelf some years ago thinking that they would be too expensive, require too much energy or that others would laugh at them. You have only one lifetime. You can't save your dreams for the next lifetime. Your dreams don't have to go onto a billboard in order for you to work on them. The key is that **you** must clearly know what is in your vision. It will **not** come about until you can articulate the vision. Even then, some of it won't occur. But knowing clearly what is in that vision will do much to increase the possibilities. Don't let your thoughts as you approach the time of your death, however far into the future that might be, include any remorse that you did not have the courage to act on your vision.

How do you write a vision? Let's start with a pad of paper and a pen or pencil. Sit down at a desk or table. You need good lighting and a straight-backed chair (don't get too comfortable). Put your name and the date on the paper along with "This is my vision statement." Not too difficult so far, is it?

Next think about all the things, regardless of whether you think you can accomplish them on your income or with your time or other restraints that you face, that ideally would be accomplished by you or with your assistance. This might include seeing your child get a graduate degree, a goal which obviously would be done primarily by that child some day. But you would have to help set the stage. What about projects in which you are already involved? Where would you like them to lead to in the long run? What about your family, your church, your friends, your ideas? Write down what comes to your mind. Later you will have the opportunity to go back and polish up the page. Right now you need to get your thoughts down on paper. What is your dream? What is your vision?

Once your thoughts are recorded on paper, put your list away in a secure place (make a copy and store it in a different place like in a safety deposit box). Return to it another day to improve upon it and add other things that will come to mind after this moment. Remember that this is for you. It is not something you will publish (although you might want to share it with others). This is your vision statement. Look at it at least once a year. Make refinements as needed. Most of all, think about it. The more you think about it, the greater will be the portion that becomes reality some day.

Writing A Personal Mission Statement

People often ask, "What is the difference between a vision statement and a mission statement?" Your vision is your dream, the ideal you would like to be able to see some day. Your mission is the portion of the vision on which you are currently acting. It is your manifesto. Your personal mission, your reason for being, is wrapped up in this statement.

The second most often asked question is, "Why do I need to write it down?" There are two reasons. First, the process of writing it down will be a meaningful experience in itself. As you struggle with writing your mission you will force yourself to articulate clearly what it is that you are trying to say. What you keep in your head can remain clear in some parts and fuzzy in others. When you decide to commit it to paper, you will be forced to be more succinct, clearer and articulate.

Second, you then have a written record of your mission. This allows you to look at it again and again. You can make a copy that you carry with you, that you put in front of you at your desk or workbench or kitchen. Having a copy that you look at will constantly remind you of your mission. This will help your concentration as you make decisions every minute of your life as to whether that decision will help or hinder you from realizing your mission.

Think of your mission statement as an integrated "to-do list" from which you work during the day. There is no one way to prepare it. Some will write it in fine prose. Others will prefer a list. The form is not the concern. The mission must be readable and comprehensible. It must be something that motivates you when you look at it.

A colleague of mine, Dr. Richard Smith, has suggested that a "To Do" list should be a "To Do/To Be" list. On your list you should add those things that will help you to become the person your value system suggests you want to be some day.

Those of you familiar with business literature today know that a fair amount has been written about mission statements for organizations. The concept is certainly a valid one for organizations as well as individuals. But part of that literature says that a mission statement must be very brief so that everyone can memorize, can recite, can be constantly motivated by this static statement.

A personal mission statement, however, should not be a slogan or a brief statement that will summarize your goals. A personal mission statement should include all of your major, current projects. You do not need to include every detail here (there is room for detail in other places), but your statement should be sufficient to drive you onward by including the major sections of each activity.

The next step is for you to write a personal mission statement. What drives you from day to day? What are the goals you are trying to accomplish? They might be as mundane as to put food on the table, or they could be as broad as to improve the life conditions for a group of people. Whatever they are, put them down on paper. Be guided by your Christian faith as you write. What would God want you to be doing? The act of writing the mission statement can itself be a revitalizing force in your life.

Setting Specific Goals: The Framework

This chapter introduces the concept of writing personal and professional goals. The framework for these goals was introduced above. Any personal or professional goal must flow from a vision statement and then a mission statement. If the goal is inconsistent with these statements or, even if it is not mentioned there, that goal is inappropriate. You might correct an inconsistency by adding something to the mission statement (and maybe the vision statement), but the three (vision, mission, goal) **must be consistent with one another.**

What Is A Goal?

A goal is something that we want to have happen in a given time frame. In addition, we are willing to commit time, energy and other resources toward its accomplishment and have the focus, courage and skill to face obstacles that, if not overcome, would prevent it from happening.

Are All Goals Equal?

Not all goals are equal in importance. Some are very important, some are important and some are just desirable.

Not all goals are equal in their urgency. Some are very urgent, some are urgent and some should be done some time.

Not all goals are equal in the drive behind them. Some goals are set forth by highly motivated and skilled people, some goals are set forth by people who would really like to see the goal accomplished and some goals are set forth by people who feel getting the goal accomplished would be nice. Many goals have some of each of these categories behind them. No goal will be accomplished unless at least one person is highly motivated and skilled.

Now, think about the possible combinations of goals with these three characteristics. Which ones are the most likely to get done? You're right. Those with the highest motivation and skill behind them.

Goals will differ in importance and urgency. But the goals with human motivation and skill behind them are the ones most likely to get done regardless of whether they are the most important. So a very important goal that is urgent has little chance of success until someone with motivation and skill gets behind it to ensure its success. It is the person behind a goal that matters.

What Do You Want To See Happen?

Let's assume you are motivated and have the necessary skills to see that your goals are accomplished. The big question for you, then, is what goals do you wish to set? Goals are set on the basis of your values. What, within your value system, is not what you would like it to be? Once you identify this, you are ready to begin the process of goal setting. What change do you want? What do you want to accomplish? What is left undone in your life? What promises have you made to God, others or yourself in which you said, "Someday I'll do this"? Be open and honest with yourself.

This is one of those times when a pad of paper and a pen can be very handy. Try writing down thoughts that come to your mind as you answer the questions at the end of the last paragraph. Once you have completed everything that comes to mind, look at what is on the paper. How many of the goals are related? How many are dependent upon other goals? A goal is dependent upon other goals if it is impossible to begin action on it until other things are accomplished. What must be accomplished first? What are these other goals? Write them down as well.

Then you might let your spouse or a close friend look at your rough draft. What things strike them as missing or strange? If the person you have asked to read the list is surprised by a goal you have written down, why is that? What is surprising about it? Did you state your goal as you intended? How do you feel about it? Note the modifications that this process has prompted you to consider.

What Categories of Goals?

The goals you have noted so far probably fall into several categories. If your goals include both personal and professional issues, you will probably want to write them on two separate pages. To help you with goal writing, the following is a suggestion of some categories you might want to include. Some of these might suggest others that apply to you or maybe modifications of these to fit your circumstances:

Personal Goals	Professional Goals
Spouse	Current Job Description
Children	Company changes
Family, Parents, Grandparents	Education
Friends	Experience/Qualifications
Home/Housing	Possible Promotions
Hobbies/Special Interests	Career Changes
Church	Christian Witness
Community Leader	Major Projects
Major Personal Project	Minor Projects

Making A Difference

Have you ever grumbled about the way something was done by others, about something in your community that you oppose, about a problem that you continually observe? Are you willing to set a goal to do something about your concerns? What would happen if you became involved in one or more of those issues?

What about things that you really like? Could you improve on any of them? Are any of them being threatened or challenged by changes in society? Maybe you could do something to protect that which you cherish.

What about your talents, abilities and spiritual gifts? See Chapter Four for more background on this issue. If you have a spiritual gift that you are not utilizing, what about a goal related to how you will begin to use it? What about your talents? How might you use them to make a difference in society?

Your Christian Influence

As a Christian you are different from non-Christians. Would people who are around you be surprised to learn that you are a Christian? If the answer to this is yes, what does that say about your Christian influence? If the answer to this is no, what is the influence you are having? What goals have you set that you are currently working on concerning the influence of your Christian faith?

Much of the influence a Christian has on others is through his or her behavior model. If you let people know you are a Christian, they will watch to see how you behave in trying circumstances (a crisis) and in very ordinary circumstances (do you put money in the cup for the soda you took from the company refrigerator?). Yet Christians who reason that their influence will be only through their behavior are missing the opportunity to set goals that could have a dramatic effect. Matthew 28:18-20 is not passive; it is very aggressive in stating the responsibility Christians have to assume a positive influence on the world.

A Draft Set Of Goals

By now you should be ready to have a draft set of goals for your personal life and, if you are actively employed, for your professional life. It will likely look very rough at this point, but it is a beginning. Some goals will overlap and that is good because your personal and professional lives are in fact related. If you have not yet written anything down concerning your goals, why not set this book down now, take out the pad of paper and pen or pencil and start the effort? It might help to read back through the past several pages to give you some ideas on getting this effort started.

Once you have a draft set of goals, keep it handy so that you can add to it as you think of other goals to add. Most of us have many half-developed goals in our heads that we have not clearly stated or maybe never even have mentioned to anyone else. As we go through the week something will remind us of another thought we have had about something we would like to see happen. Might this be formulated into another goal?

Your goals are never finished. There is always the opportunity to add more goals, refine others and mark others off as completed. Goal setting is a dynamic rather than a static process.

A Priority For Every Goal

In Chapter Seven we will devote some attention to the setting of priorities. Every goal that you set must be prioritized in relationship to the other goals. Some goals are clearly more important than others; some goals are clearly more urgent than others. Your success personally or at work is heavily dependent upon your ability to know the difference between a goal of great importance and one of considerable importance. In addition your success rests upon your ability to distinguish between a goal that must be done as quickly as possible and another goal that is very important.

At times it appears that all goals are extremely important and all need immediate action. It is in times like these that those who are highly successful will make the right choices. Part of it is not buckling under pressure and part of it is knowing which of the important goals gets the priority for now and which of the urgent goals gets the priority for now. This requires knowledge, skill, perspective and experience plus high motivation and focus upon what is significant.

A Strategy For Every Goal

At this point you have established your vision statement, your mission statement, your set of goals and are beginning to set the priorities among your goals. The remaining step is setting a strategy for accomplishing each prioritized goal. See

Chapter Seven for more information about determining strategies, including why writing effective strategies is so important.

Strategies make the difference between a noble statement of a goal and the accomplishment of that goal. It is all part of a system to which you must make a commitment in order to have an important impact upon the world around you.

A Time Frame For Every Goal

One part of setting priorities as noted above is recording the appropriate timing for getting something done. Every goal at its conception has a time frame in mind. As we set priorities we make decisions about which goals should be addressed first, second and last. Such decisions are important. Part of this is because many goals are dependent upon certain other goals being done first and because not all goals have the same urgency. It is essential to be able to evaluate that urgency so that goals are met in some relationship to their urgency.

Measuring Goal Accomplishment

Many goals are accomplished with one act. They are either done or not done. As we mature, however, our goals are likely to become more complex. Complex goals are likely to have subparts. This means that goals could be partly accomplished. To the extent to which the subparts of a goal are done at different times, involve different people, have different strategies or have different priorities, they need to be listed separately in our lists.

Complex goals that do not lend themselves to being separated into two or more goals are those which require evaluative monitoring. How are you doing on this goal? Are you honest with yourself about your progress? How does it relate to your timetable? Be careful that some small part that you subconsciously avoid does not prevent the goal from being accomplished.

Revisiting Personal/Professional Goals Annually

As noted earlier in this chapter, personal and professional goals are not static once written. They are subject to revisions continually as you add new goals, rewrite existing goals and check off goals that you have accomplished. These goals should be kept with you in a clipboard, purse, briefcase, computer case or other item that travels with you. Review the goals often to keep them in mind. Goals kept in mind are more likely to be accomplished.

Even when you carry your goals with you most of the time and look at them often, it is still recommended that you set a regular time each year (like January 1st) to sit down and look at your complete set of goals and reflect upon changes during the past year. This is the process of stepping back to get a bigger picture of what is happening in your life. By doing this you will see things happening in your goal structure that might not be apparent when you look at the set of goals each day.

Having A Passion For Our Vision, Mission And Goals

You might say, "This all sounds good, but is it worth all the effort I will have to invest in it?" If your attitude toward the goal-setting process is one of duty rather than excitement, it probably won't be worth it. However, if you are excited about the impact your life can have upon the lives of others and how you can accomplish so much by this planning process, then it will have a positive impact and you won't even notice the effort you have expended in making it happen. Life is much more fun when you plan for it, devote effort to making things happen and do this on the basis of a value system that is undergirded with a strong Christian faith.

Chapter Seven

Development Of Priorities: What Is Most Important?

Though cultures differ and times change, the Word of our God stands forever as an unchanging source of answers to all of life's problems. — Billy Graham[1]

It is more urgent today than ever that we try to understand the dynamics of renewal. — Robert H. Waterman, Jr.[2]

In today's world and Church, disciplined Christian lives are the exception, not the rule. — Kent Hughes[3]

Priorities are a matter both of determining the relative importance in the accomplishment of goals and determining the optimum time frame in which to accomplish those goals. The most important priority is not necessarily the one we complete first, but the most important priority must always be done, done well, on a timely basis, as promised.

Reviewing The Goals: What Is Urgent? What Is Important?

The setting of priorities is meaningless until we have set goals. In an earlier chapter the subject of goals was addressed. As a result, it is hoped that you have formulated some goals. Some of these will be short-term and others long-term goals. Some goals will be important. Some goals must be accomplished as soon as possible. Some goals depend upon the work of others; others depend only on us. Some goals require a great deal of time or money and maybe other resources.

But every goal requires that we set priorities among our goals and develop a strategy (or strategies) to accomplish them. In the next chapter we will talk about strategies. At this point we need to determine our priorities.

If we have forty-seven goals, for example, most of them will have a unique set of the characteristics mentioned in the first paragraph above. Some will be short-term and others long-term. Some will be more important than others. Some are more timely. Sorting out priorities is essential. Without setting priorities, we will accomplish few of our goals and then likely not to a satisfactory extent or quality.

So how do we approach the setting of priorities? Stephen R. Covey has suggested a simple classification of priorities:[4]

I. Important, Urgent	II. Important, Not Urgent
III. Not Important, Urgent	IV. Not Important, Not Urgent

Every goal can be placed in one of these categories. For example, a goal might move from Section I to Section II as the result of completing some of the most urgent aspects of that goal even though not all aspects of the goal have been completed (maybe some are now waiting upon other people to do something). Some goals become more important or more urgent because of changing circumstances, one of which might be that we did not complete the goal earlier and now it has become a larger issue. Goals are never static (as opposed to dynamic) because life is never static. Even when we do nothing, life around us continues to change at an amazing pace.

EXERCISE

Using a sheet of paper, draw a large diagram similar to the Covey diagram above and place each of the goals you developed in Chapter Six into one of the four categories.

After you have completed the exercise, look at the overall picture of where you have placed your goals in the categories. Now, answer the following questions:

- How realistic is your chart? Consider adjusting it now to reflect what you think you can realistically place in either the **important** or **urgent** categories.

- What percentage of your goals are now in one of the two **important** sections?

- What percentage of your goals are now in one of the two **urgent** sections?

- This chart gives you a rough draft of your priorities. What do you think of the priorities before you?

- Are you willing to address your goals with this structure of priorities? If not, what penalties are you willing to accept?

- Are your priorities feasible? Can they be done with the amount of energy you are willing to invest?

- What is the likely impact that the priorities you have set will have on others? Any reactions to be expected?

- What resources are required to address the first few priorities? Do you have those resources? If not, how will you get them?

Urgent First

By placing your goals into the four categories, you are saying that your first priorities are those which you placed in Section I. Section III would be next because those priorities deal with what needs to be done next. Section III is less important than Section II, but the items you placed there are urgent. You need to be sure they are really urgent. Taking out the garbage when the garbage truck is expected during the next twenty minutes might be urgent but not as important as many other things you must do.

However, you will do the urgent item now so that you can then address the important but not urgent. Important but not Urgent (Section II) items will move to the Important and Urgent category if not addressed within a reasonable amount of time. It is best to deal with them before they move to the urgent category. You might be thinking that it would be good to keep all things from getting into the urgent side of the box. That would be the ideal. However, emergencies, procrastination, time demands by others, underestimating the size of a task and other factors will still push items into the left side of the box.

Anxiety

We tend to experience anxiety proportionate to the number of items that are in the left side of the box. Consequently, anxiety is reduced as the left side of the box is emptied. We cannot keep it empty, but we will reduce our anxiety if we keep it as empty as possible. Some important and urgent things, like giving a speech or presentation, cannot be done in advance. There is only one time for it. But we can still reduce the anxiety related to it by being as prepared as possible. Much of the anxiety related to a particular event in our lives can be traced to our inadequate preparation for the event. Anxiety is also produced by lack of experience, by unfamiliarity. Anxiety is reduced when we repeat a prior successful experience.

Related to this is the consideration that we can best relate to the important but not urgent items if the left side of the box is virtually empty. We are not distracted either directly or indirectly (including our consciences telling us that we really should be working on an urgent matter) from an important but not urgent task if the urgent items in our lives are essentially cared for at the time we begin to address the important but not urgent task.

Some of you might respond to this by saying, "I have an ongoing, important and urgent item that is never fully cared for at any time." An example of this might be caring for a handicapped child or a parent who lives in your home and is not fully capable of caring for himself or herself. Depending upon how much this situation demands of you and how much it is likely to produce an emergency at any given moment, you should still try to reduce as much of this responsibility to routine as possible. Rather than assuming more responsibility for his or her life than is required, leave as much as is medically and psychologically possible with the individual. Be sure that you do not diminish the person's self-respect by doing a task that he or she is capable of doing. Yet, the bottom line is the responsibility that you have for that person.

Attitude

When you assume the responsibility for a task that requires you to do things for others, including raising children, the enormity of the task is closely related to your attitude about the task. Examine your attitude. If you intensely resent the task, such as caring for a physically impaired child, examine your feelings deeply, preferably with another adult you respect, who is not affected by the same situation, to determine why you feel the way you do. You might be creating your own anxieties by your attitude about why you are the one to provide the care or maybe about why the care is needed in the first place. An attitude that allows you to deal openly and honestly with deep-seated anxieties can result in a new freedom, a new release in your life.

On To Section II

In the above discussion we dealt with the urgent, the left side of the box. This included both the important and not so important. But all these goals were urgent. The point was made that we need to move from caring for the left side so that we can successfully deal with the important but not urgent. If we successfully manage ourselves throughout life, most of our activity will be in Section II. We are likely to do our best work here. While some of us work best, or least reason or rationalize that we do, under pressure, that might simply be because we are always finding ourselves working under pressure and we produce what is needed because of the reward or the penalty.

Section II will likely include both short-term and long-term goals. Which ones do we tackle first? That is partly a matter of choice and partly a matter of our track records. When we tackle the short-term goals first, do our track records show that we often never get to the long-term goals? Or to put it the other way around, when we tackle the long-term goals first, do we ever find time for the short-term goals? Remember, success in all aspects of life is related to balance and focus. While there is more on this in other parts of the book, remember that balance requires us to focus on the matter at hand while paying attention to how that goal relates to other goals, and this includes knowing when to move to another goal because of the matter of balance in our lives. Our priority lists always include things we really enjoy doing and other activities we dislike. Our success depends upon getting both sets of goals done on a timely and quality basis in a manner that brings satisfaction to others affected by the goals and ourselves.

Priorities Within A Section

Not all goals within a section are equal in either importance or urgency. Once you complete the exercise above in which you place all your goals into one of the four sections, you are able to sift through a section and determine what the priorities should be within that section. Some goals might almost as well fit into the adjacent section. I suggest that you sort the goals within each section now.

Some goals can be of equal importance. Do not spend a great deal of time making narrow distinctions between several goals. Remember that some goals will be best accomplished simultaneously. After starting on one project, you might need to wait for materials, for another person to do something or for the weather to change. During that time you can start another project (working a goal toward realization).

Some of us are better than others at keeping several balls in the air at the same time. My wife Jackie is a master at keeping many balls in the air at the same time while she prepares one of her wonderful feasts such as for Christmas or a family birthday. The rolls can be baking while the carrots are cooking but both have to be watched in order to make sure they are not overdone and that they reach their peak all at about the same time so that we can all sit down, including Jackie, at the same time to eat.

I personally enjoy having many balls in the air at the same time. I see it as a means of getting more goals accomplished because success in so many of them is dependent upon other people and events. It also provides variety. You need to examine yourself to determine how many balls you are comfortable with having in the air at the same time. You will not be successful if you attempt more goals at the same time than you are comfortable in handling. Few of us can afford the luxury of working on a single goal at a time. What we find ourselves doing in that case is having a large goal that then gets broken down into many smaller goals.

Priorities As A Reflection Of Our Values

As we set our goals and as we set priorities among our goals, we remain conscious of our value systems. We will neither set goals nor priorities within those goals that are inconsistent with our value systems. The person who attempts to do this is confused and faces an internal paradox. That is, any person who attempts to do something that is inconsistent with his or her values will find internal conflict that often finds its outlet in anger that is directed towards others or self-destruction.

In a very real sense, none of us ever acts outside of our value systems. What we sometimes do, however, is take action or say something that is based upon a lower value than the one that is primary to that situation, an action that is inconsistent with our values ranking. For example, I value my wife and our relationship, but I also value a particular magazine. I might conclude that the magazine is missing and confront my wife in a manner suggesting that she was the one who caused the disappearance of the magazine (whether or not she did is not the issue at this point). In so doing, I am placing my value for the magazine above my value for my wife. If I were asked which of the two values is the most important, I would always say, "my wife." Yet my action in this example is inconsistent with the ranking of my values. When I return to my senses (the issue of my magazine is no longer an emotional issue for me), I realize that I probably did not act as I should have and I, hopefully, apologize. I acted within my value system but outside of my values ranking.

As we set priorities within our value systems, we also have the opportunity to set these priorities in a manner that is consistent with our values. Let's say that on a given Monday evening you are late coming home from work (or maybe playing golf), you promised one of your children that you would do something with him or her which might take fifteen to twenty minutes, you have a meeting at church you promised to attend, your spouse wants to talk about something that happened at work today, the garbage must be taken out to the road and you have an article that is must reading before leaving for work in the morning. Let's say you consider all of these important and urgent. You want to be sure to meet the goal of satisfying each need, and all of them must be done before going to bed that night and in a quality manner. How do you sort out such priorities? Do you do the most important one first? If so, which one is the most important? Let's look at this situation closely to analyze your options and fit each goal into a priority order that is consistent with your value systems.

Setting priorities is not just a matter of what do we do first. It is also a matter of looking at the time frame in which something can be accomplished. As we analyze each of the goals in the paragraph above, we assume that you are home at 6:15 p.m. and dinner is ready to be served. Dinner will take thirty minutes, the meeting at church is at 7:30, requiring departure by 7:15 and a return by 9:30 p.m. Which of the items has no flexibility, and which of them has some flexibility?

The meeting at the church has no time flexibility other than that of arriving late or leaving early, neither of which is a good alternative. Dinner, too, cannot be delayed and cannot be missed. This then means that 6:15 to 6:45 and 7:15 to 9:30 are committed to nonflexible goals. You have from 6:45 to 7:15 and 9:30 until bedtime to prioritize to meet the remaining goals. You have four remaining goals:

1. Spending about fifteen to twenty minutes with one of your children,
2. Hearing what your spouse has to say about work today,
3. Reading the article, and
4. Taking the garbage out to the road.

Can you devise a strategy to do all four in a quality manner? Here are some of the possibilities you might consider:

1. You might ask your spouse if the work matter could be discussed over dinner or maybe after returning from the church meeting when the two of you have some quiet time after the children have gone to bed.

2. You might ask your child if he or she is ready with the activity you planned to do together. If so, getting to it quickly after dinner might be a good choice unless your spouse has indicated that he or she must have that time frame. Alternatively, depending upon the age of the child, you might do this activity after returning from the church meeting.

3. That article. Since it relates to no one else in the household, it will probably get last priority. You could fit it into any time slot (or maybe parts of several), or it could be done after everyone has gone to bed. You could also plan to get up extra early tomorrow morning to read it then.

4. Taking the garbage out to the road might most easily be done as you go out of the house on the way to the church for the meeting.

All during this time there will be other less demanding activities. Helping load the dishwasher, talking with other children, returning a phone call from a friend, looking at the newspaper and replacing a burned-out light bulb. Exasperating? Not if you organize your priorities (schedule your time to meet each goal that is prioritized to be met in this time frame) and if you have confidence in your ability to handle a number of balls in the air at one time.

Note that every one of these goals in the example was consistent with your values system. However, the goals were vying for the same priority—they all needed to be addressed during a relatively short time frame. As we will discuss in the next section, it is essential that you personally remain in control of setting your priorities. While you can be sensitive to how others feel about their interaction with you on one or more of your goals, you need to develop a plan whereby you can prioritize the accomplishment of your goals with a sequence plan for a given segment of time.

The Process Of Setting Priorities

There are several steps to address before moving along to establish priorities. These steps are:

- Possessing a reasonably high self-esteem, being at peace with God (your Christian faith is sound), being at peace with yourself, and having a knowledge of both your spiritual gifts and your God-given talents. The more optimum these factors are, the better you will do at setting goals and priorities.

- Developing a written set of goals such as we covered in Chapter Six.

- Determining priority sections for the goals using the Covey diagram that was introduced at the beginning of the chapter or another configuration that satisfies your circumstance.

- Determining the relative importance and relative urgency of the goals inside of each section.

- Placing yourself firmly in charge of deciding your goals and your priorities while considering your Christian faith, your value system, and the needs and desires of others who will be affected by your decisions. In this way you are also responsible for what you do, for the results of your decisions about goals and priorities.

That a reasonably high self-esteem, being at peace with God (your Christian faith is sound), being at peace with yourself and having a knowledge of both your spiritual gifts and your God-given talents is number one on the list might be a surprise to you. It is here on the assumption that you cannot write reasonable goals reflecting your Christian faith and character and do so in a meaningful way for yourself unless this platform requirement is met. If you have not successfully addressed these issues in your life, seek out others you respect and talk it through with them before concluding where you are and what you should do about it. Having your platform in good shape is like laying a firm foundation when building a building. Beautiful brickwork is meaningless when the foundation under it crumbles.

Once the platform is established as reasonably firm, the second step is to write a set of goals such as we covered in Chapter Six. Consider the guidance in this chapter, and then prepare written goals that, while being written primarily for yourself, can be understood by others.

The third step is to determine the relative importance and relative urgency of the goals inside of each section. This requires you to complete the exercise at the beginning of this chapter and consider the guidance which follows the exercise.

Fourth, you must place yourself firmly in charge of deciding your goals and your priorities while considering your Christian faith, your value system and the needs and desires of others who will be affected by your decisions. This is not just a fourth step in the sequence. It is more like part of the platform. It must undergird your whole approach to the task of setting personal, professional and other goals and priorities.

Keeping Vision And Mission In Perspective

In Chapter Six we introduced the concept of a personal vision statement and a personal mission statement. In summary, what we said was that each person should have a personal vision statement and a personal mission statement. A vision is what you might some day be, the dreams of a future day. A mission is what has been decided upon already, a compilation of the goals that you are working on today. If you have no vision, no dream, it will certainly not just happen. Great things in the world begin with a vision in someone's mind and heart.

At the same time, each of us needs to focus on a mission. We accomplish little without a mission, without a focus. A mission tells us why we exist. Our focus says, "This is what I will do to the exclusion of other things I might do." We might call this our mission focus. It causes us to exclude some things from our lives because they are not important to our mission focus, we do not have time to include them, we do not have an interest in them, they are not consistent with our spiritual gifts and God-given talents and other reasons. That leaves us with our mission focus. In Chapter Six you were given the opportunity to develop your mission focus.

Vision and mission are mentioned in this chapter again because of their relationship to setting priorities. Because our priorities are a result of sorting our goals into categories and then determining what must be done first, this sorting must constantly be tested against our vision and mission focuses. Our visions include possible future goals while our mission focuses encompass the goals we hold today. In setting priorities it is tempting to include items that others might want us to do, and sometimes they get incorporated into our goals because we want to please others (more on this in the next section). It is also tempting to wander through life without regard to what we really want to accomplish. Our priorities must be based upon our mission focuses rather than on a random motive that presents itself (someone suggests doing something, we see something interesting, we see something that should be done by someone). Having a mission focus helps us to set priorities for only those things that are goals we have set that fall within our mission focuses for today. We might add things to our visions, or we might make our visions clearer. We might move things from our visions to our mission focuses. But we still need to set only those priorities that fall within our mission focuses as we define them today.

Priorities And Other People

Most goals within our mission focuses deal with people (both ourselves and others). Even goals that are not primarily people-oriented, like improving our natural environments, are probably included because of our desires to improve the environment's effect on people, and our work will certainly help people. Goals and priorities, then, can be divided into:

- self (including our relationships with God),
- other people,
- things.

Some might feel that God should be considered as a separate category. The reason God is not in a separate category is because we are talking in this book about effective personal management. We do not manage God. We have no goals for God to accomplish. We have no priorities for God to set. Now there are things we pray to God for, asking that He do this or that. But I cannot think of a prayer that we might pray in which we ask for something that is not primarily for the benefit of one of the three categories above. We do pray that God's name be glorified, that He be exalted. We pray prayers of thanksgiving. I am suggesting that this is because of our relationships to God which is included in category one. If you are uncomfortable with this, then simply create four categories as you examine your priorities.

Much of this book is about category one above, self, including our relationships with God. At this point, however, I would like for us to focus upon the second category, priorities that relate to other people.

None of us lives on an island by himself or herself without contact with other people. Even in the process of reading this book we establish contact with another human being. Much of what we do every day is activity that is done with others or for others. And much of the rest of human activity is action by others for us, for others. We are really a very dependent people. Our increasingly complex society makes this even more true every day.

What does the Bible say about our relationships with others? Jesus said, "So in everything, do to others what you would have them do to you, for this sums up the Law and the Prophets."[5] Paul advised the church at Ephesus:

Therefore each of you must put off falsehood and speak truthfully to his neighbor, for we are all members of one body. In your anger do not sin: Do not let the sun go down while you are still angry, and do not give the devil a foothold. He who has been stealing must steal no longer, but must work, doing something useful with his own hands, that he may have something to share with those in need. Do not let any unwholesome talk come out of your mouths, but only what is helpful for building others up according to their needs, that it may benefit those who listen. And do not grieve the Holy Spirit of God, with whom you were sealed for the day of redemption. Get rid of all bitterness, rage and anger, brawling and slander, along with every form of malice. Be kind and compassionate to one another, forgiving each other, just as in Christ God forgave you.[6]

The New Testament emphasizes our devotion to others, to whom we should show empathy, love, compassion and support. We are told to do for others even to the denial of self. As Christians this becomes imbedded into our value systems. Because our goals (our mission focus) come from our value systems, this concern for others gets carried over into our goals. From there it is carried over into our priorities and then into our daily behavior or actions.

Since most goals, and hence priorities, fall into one of the first two categories, let's focus here upon the second category, others and our relationship with them. While volumes have been written about this and many are listed in the bibliography of this book for your ease in finding them, our attention here is on how our mission focus (goals) relates to others.

One way to give attention to this is to take our complete sets of goals and organize them according to this framework. This would mean listing together all goals that relate primarily to self, all goals that relate primarily to others and all goals that relate primarily to things. This could help us to see how our goals that relate to others tie together, to determine how well they are consistent with one another and the extent to which they might overlap.

You have heard others refer to the "servant's heart," and possibly you have used that term yourself. Paul advised Timothy, "And the Lord's servant must not quarrel; instead, he must be kind to everyone, able to teach, not resentful."[7] What does it mean? List three characteristics of a person with a "servant's heart."

- _____

- _____

- _____

Now look at these characteristics. How well do they describe you? All of the time? Some of the time? Having a "servant's heart" is partly a matter of values (other people are important and I must help them) and partly a matter of attitudes (no one wants my help; or help me, God, to find other ways to serve others). Examine both as you look at how well you fit the descriptors you wrote in above.

If you are a Christian (we are told to love one another[8]) and if you are other-person centered (have a servant's heart), you will be interested in how your goals (mission focus) affect others. You will write your goals with others in mind, and you will carry them out (setting priorities) by giving paramount importance to their impact upon others.

Maintaining Balance

Priorities deal with both timing (when to do it) and importance (what would happen if it doesn't get done). Neither can be considered to the exclusion of the other. Priorities also must stem from goals. We take action for a reason, not just to fill time or to act out an impulse. If we use our time, financial and other resources wisely, we will maintain a balance in the setting of our priorities. This balance must consider our goals (mission focus) and their underlying values as well as their timing and importance.

Important and urgent tasks might need to be interrupted by the important but not urgent issues. Taking a call from a son or daughter who wants to tell you Happy Birthday or to have a nice day when you are in the midst of a major activity is one example. Balance comes from having a focus. Hanging in there with the important and urgent activity even though you are interrupted requires balance in your priorities. You must know that if one ball has to drop, which one it cannot be. For instance, balance might mean picking up the dry cleaning as you go by the cleaners today even though you don't need the clothes right now because later it would mean a special trip and cause the dry cleaning to become an urgent issue at that time.

Values, including our Christian faith, accompanied by a mission focus and carefully set priorities are all part of a balance that will allow each of us to serve God according to our spiritual gifts and God-given talents, have an impact on others through serving them and bring satisfaction to our own lives through meaningful accomplishments.

Footnotes

[1]Billy Graham, *Answers to Life's Problems· Guidance For Personal Decisions.* Foreword by Richard C. Halverson (Dallas, TX: Word Publishing, 1988), pp. 9-10.

[2]Robert H. Waterman, Jr., *The Renewal Factor: How The Best Get And Keep The Competitive Edge* (New York, NY: Bantam Books, 1987), p. 1.

[3]Kent Hughes, *Disciplines of a Godly Man* (Wheaton, IL: Crossway Books, 1991), p. 17.

[4]Stephen R. Covey, *The Seven Habits of Highly Effective People: Restoring the Character Ethic* (New York, NY: Simon and Schuster, 1989), p. 151.

[5]Matthew 7:12.

[6]Ephesians 4:25-32.

[7]2 Timothy 2:24.

[8]"Dear friends, let us love one another, for love comes from God. Everyone who loves has been born of God and knows God. Whoever does not love does not know God, because God is love.... Dear friends, since God so loved us, we also ought to love one another. No one has ever seen God; but if we love one another, God lives in us and his love is made complete in us" (1 John 4:7-8, 11-12).

Chapter Eight

Setting Strategies

Reviewing Our Progress

In Chapters One to Seven you were introduced to the concept of assuming control and responsibility for your life through explaining the prerequisites for that action, exploring what it means to be you (Chapter Two), what it means to be a Christian (Chapter Three), what talents, abilities, spiritual gifts and education you have to equip you for the journey (Chapter Four), understanding the values you have (Chapter Five), setting goals that are consistent with those values (Chapter Six) and then developing priorities (Chapter Seven). This leads us to this chapter in which we will explore the concept of setting strategies for those goals that are consistent with your priorities.

Values

You will recall that your values are those things you hold dear. You might not understand why some things are valued and some values might be inconsistent with other values, but they are your values. You believe in them and you try to guide your life by them. You would have a hard time putting them into a list according to their importance to you but they have a relative importance, nonetheless. You might discover their relative importance when you go looking for a new car. Having a dependable car with the latest technology that will look good to others is important to you, but you also value having a savings account. Right now you have, in effect, said the car is the greater value to you. But you ease your conscience by rationalizing that you won't use your savings for the car and the amount you have financed is just like a lease.

Vision

Each of us has a vision as well. For many of us it is very clouded, but there is still a vision. For others it is the daily guide of what they wish to construct in this life. Our vision, therefore, is our ideal. If we could only achieve our dreams with all the barriers lifted, here is the world we would create. Some of that vision is likely to come about; other parts will remain only a vision throughout the rest of our lives. Our vision changes as we achieve adult status and keeps changing some after that. Our vision will take into account the reality of life so far; when it doesn't, we are just daydreaming. There is a significant difference. Daydreaming is an escape. Our vision is where we would like to be some day.

Mission

All of us like to pull bits of our visions into our missions. It is here that we see realistic and attainable goals, a life that we could attain with the right amount of work and focus. We are guided by our missions even if we cannot express them well in writing. We can talk about our visions even if they are inconsistent and they change some from day to day. Those of us who are most likely to attain our missions are those who can keep their missions in focus and who are willing to devote the energy as well as their talents, spiritual gifts and abilities to achieve these missions.

Goals

To achieve a mission we develop specific goals. These goals are action oriented. By accomplishing them we move closer to our missions. Our goals must guide our actions every day. Goals must be written in order to be effective.

Before getting to the chapter on strategies, we have set some goals and determined priorities among those goals. The goals tell what we want to accomplish, and the priorities tell us which of these goals are the most to the least important. Together they tell us where to start. Generally we will want to deal with what is both important and urgent. This will be a goal with a high priority, a priority that says it cannot wait until most other things are done.

Priorities

We cannot complete all of our goals the first day. Priorities allow us to decide where to start—to identify the goals that should get our attention right now. They are not necessarily the most important goals; in fact, some of the lesser goals must be done before the larger, more important goals can be accomplished. Priorities give us an order to our actions.

Some of us have many goals. There are many things we want to see get done. This will mean many priorities for there will be as many priorities as there are goals. There is no inherent goodness in having only a few goals or in having many. The number and types of goals must fit our opportunities, talents, health, spiritual gifts, skills and our ambitions. Some of these, such as ambition, skills and opportunities, are things we can affect. Although we do not control the existence of our spiritual gifts and talents, we do control their development and application.

Strategies

Now that we have these goals and have set priorities among them (see prior chapters), we are now ready to tackle the matter of determining strategies. Essentially what this says is, I want to accomplish certain things. Among my goals these are the most important, and now I must determine **how** I will go about accomplishing these highest priority goals. How I do them is called a strategy.

Our strategies put our priorities into plans that have a chance of getting accomplished. A goal, even a goal and its priority, will not get done without an accompanying strategy. Thus, to have goals and priorities within those goals is insufficient. We must also have strategies. This brings us to the thrust of Chapter Eight, Setting Strategies.

What Is A Strategy?

A strategy is a plan, a method of getting something done. Every goal must have one or more strategies that we will follow, or we will not accomplish our goals.

Every goal has a priority. The priority determines how the goal relates in importance and urgency to the other goals. Every goal also must have one or more strategies. The strategy determines how the goal will be accomplished. Regardless of priority, a goal will likely have at least several strategies. Priority tells importance, but strategy tells us how. A strategy usually has a number of parts or steps.

Step One, Understanding The Goal

A strategy for accomplishing a goal begins with understanding the goal and the obstacles to its accomplishment. If the goal has been poorly written, developing a set of strategies for its accomplishment will be difficult. The strategies might actually accomplish a different goal if the goal is poorly defined. So the first step must always be to understand the goal clearly. You might set a goal that you wish to be more like Jesus. This goal itself is too vague. What do you have in mind in becoming more like Jesus? Is this primarily in your thought process, in being close to God, in your influence upon others, in how you see yourself?

Goal Clarity

The clarity you need to set goals might cause you at this point to go back to your written goals in order to work on their wording so that you (and others secondarily) will understand just what the goal includes. This includes clarity between goals such as what is included in this goal and what related items are included in another goal. A goal needs to be written in sufficient detail to make it clearly understood. Amplification or explanation could be added to the goal but should not become part of the goal statement itself. Clarity is related to brevity. An endless dialogue is seldom clear. A goal must be clear in order to have any hope of being accomplished.

Step Two, Assessing The Tools

The first step mentioned above in strategies for accomplishing a goal is to understand the goal. Until this is done, there can be no second or next step. The second step in accomplishing any goal is an assessment of the tools at hand to make the goal happen.

If your goal is to be recognized as an accomplished musician, the second step would be to assess where you are in becoming that type of musician:

- Do I have the talent, the skills (keyboard for example), knowledge (music theory for example) and experience (how far along on the experience continuum am I)?

- What about my spiritual gifts?

- Do I have psychological (do I fear success) or physical barriers (is there a deformed finger on one hand that makes it difficult to play a keyboard) to this goal?

- What time do I have available to me to devote to this goal?

- Do I have the instruments, music books and practice space available?

An honest assessment of the tools available to you could cause you to refine your goal. This does not necessarily mean cutting the goal back. It could mean expanding the goal. Once we think about the tools we do have available to us, we might be motivated even more because we see that the task will not be as difficult as we thought or we see God's will evident in the situation.

Step Three, Addressing The Deficiencies

The next step (third step), however, depends upon the goal (or set of goals if one set of strategies fits a set of goals). This step will draw from your assessment mentioned as the second step. This step involves addressing the deficiencies. If your goal is be an accomplished musician and your assessment says you do not understand music theory, a possible next step in your overall strategy might be to study music theory either by reading books or by taking a course. Other areas of assessment will lead to the development of similar strategies. Once these strategies are clarified, it will be important to set priorities among the strategies. Should you study music theory before you learn the keyboard?

The more complex the goal, the more complex will be the set of strategies. There is no inherently evident number of strategies that is best. They must fit the situation defined by the goal. A strategy could have a dozen or more major sub-strategies. Keep in mind that some goals are very broad, so the strategies need to be very comprehensive. Goals should not be rewritten to fit strategies. Instead, goals should, in themselves, make sense. The goal must be understandable, as we noted earlier. A goal can be either simple and short range or complex and cover many future years. The strategy, or set of strategies, must fit whatever that reasonable goal requires for its accomplishment.

Step Four, Tackling The Goal

In the first three steps we have addressed the following:

1. Understanding the goal,

2. Assessing the tools,

3. Addressing the deficiencies.

Now we address the fourth step:

4. Tackling the goal.

This strategy might have many parts. It is tailored to the actual goal. There is no formula to offer because of the uniqueness of the various goals that an individual might set. In the first three steps, you are getting ready to tackle the goal. Now you are there. The goal dominates and your success in reaching the goal depends upon having the right strategies and then being able to execute them in precise relationship with the goal.

An Example: Opening Your Own Business

Let's take an example. Let's say your goal is to open your own business. In step one you would carefully examine exactly what business you have in mind (clarifying and understanding the goal). Remember that the more precise the goal, the greater the likelihood that it will be attained. If you have a vision for starting this business, now is the time to put your plan down precisely on paper and share it with others who are in a position either to support you personally (such as family and friends) or to support you in the details of the business (bankers, suppliers, leaseholders, potential employees and others). If your vision includes brown awnings on the front of a store or a product that has a particular appearance or appeal, spell it out on paper at this point.

To implement the second step you will need to look at who you are and how well equipped you are to open this business. How well have you prepared yourself for this move? Some of the questions you should be asking yourself at this point are:

1. What do I know about this type of business?

Be honest with yourself. This is not a time for expanding your ego. If you answer this on the basis of an inflated ego, you are assuring yourself that you will not succeed in this venture. If you answer this on the basis of a deflated ego, you are setting the stage for your own defeat. What do you really know about this type of business? Probably your answer will include some things you know well and others you do not understand or have no information to guide you. Remember to include both formal knowledge (college courses, training seminars) and informal education (what you have observed, read about or talked with others about in various settings).

2. Am I willing to learn from other people and from sources more knowledgeable?

If your response is that you already know what you need to start and you will be able to figure out the rest once you start or if your assumption is that you will never be able to learn enough, you are headed for trouble. The ship's captain always uses charts, even in familiar waters. Why is this?

3. If I am willing to learn, how will I go about guiding my learning process?

What is your learning strategy? If you wish to become a pharmacist, you will have to attend college and graduate school whether you want to or not. Where will you do this? How will you pay for this? How will this affect your family, your source of income? Even if a graduate degree is not required for your goal, should you take some classes? What about traveling around to consult with people who are knowledgeable to see what they think or what they do? Most people are willing to help others learn. You are complimenting them when you ask for information and their opinions. Be sure, however, that you are willing to listen. If you go into a meeting with a person from whom you might learn and spend ten minutes to two hours with that person and do not take a note pad and pen and write down some of what you are told, you are indicating to the other person that you are not very serious about learning. The human memory is unreliable; you remember only a fraction of what you are told. Written notes allow you to go back to recapture some of the essentials of that conversation. Take advantage of the opportunity to learn from others. It is less costly and much more helpful than learning the hard way through the process of blunders that could have easily been avoided.

4. What skills do I possess for this business?

You must start with an understanding of the skills required by this type of business. Which of them do you possess? Which are you willing to acquire? Examine this carefully. Consider, for example, that although you might have great skills as a salesperson, the new business will also require someone to keep track of the sales and the accounts receivable. What are your skills in this area? If your answer to this is that you will hire someone to do that work, remember two things. One is that personnel for a new business could use up your precious financial resources quickly. If you rely upon a family member, will that family member do what is needed or only what they are inclined to do? Second, you can't supervise what you do not understand. Many small businesses fail because the person who started the business did not adequately supervise the financial aspects of the business. This does not necessarily mean fraud, although it could. It means that financial skills are a necessary part of what you will need to start this business. What other skills will you need in this new business? Computer skills, heavy equipment operation skills, personnel skills in hiring, developing and retaining the right people, advertising and marketing skills and skills in dealing with government agencies are some of the other skills that you might be called upon to have.

5. **What talents and spiritual gifts do I have that relate to success in starting this business?**

Again, be honest with yourself. Neither overestimate nor underestimate your talents or spiritual gifts. Have some frank conversations with others to let them guide you tactfully in this evaluation. Listen to what they have to say. At the same time, put your own perception to work here. Not everything others say should be taken at face value. Many times the motives of others prompt them to say things that are not helpful to you. Find people who are both knowledgeable (sharing ignorance is seldom helpful) and have a reputation of wanting to help others. Asking your physician about whether you should open a store is not likely to be helpful. Asking your minister about entering some form of ministry, however, could be very helpful. The minister, on the other hand, would be limited in advising you about a career in the health professions. In this case your physician might be the guide you need.

6. **What is my motivation?**

If the challenge of starting your own business will require much of you, is it greater than your motivation will allow you to provide? If you want to achieve a major goal, there must be the corresponding major motivation. Be sure your motivation will sustain you even in the difficult times when you must face your banker to obtain capital or the potential client who turns you down. If you enter your own business, you must accept that there will be valleys as well as mountains in the conduct of that business. Be sure your motivation will sustain you through both.

One aspect of motivation is focus. When you are on the mountains in your new business, it is easy to lose focus. This is when you are tempted to branch out into other activities that are not central to your business. Any successful business remains successful only if those responsible clearly know what business they are in and then stick to that business.

7. **What do I need to know about this business in order to succeed in it?**

What strategies should you develop even before you open the business that will increase your likelihood of success? What are your goals for the business? How will you achieve those goals?

Step Five, Following Through

Strategies brought through Step Four can still fall flat (fail to succeed) unless there is follow-through. Step Four, Tackling the Goal, embodies action concerning the goal. Taking action requires courage. Action that is consistent with the values, goals and priorities of that individual is a logical conclusion to the development of those values and the setting of goals and priorities.

Deciding to take action and then doing it requires follow-through. In the follow-through stage of any action, whether business or personal, the following characteristics are present:

1. **Thorough knowledge of the steps already taken.**

Perhaps some time has elapsed since the first action, and some actions were possibly taken by several different people. At this point the person leading the follow-through should be completely aware of what has happened since the first action on the project and what action has been taken to date by all known participants in your organization. Then some recorded assessment of what this means will help in getting the larger picture of where you are in this project.

2. **Contact with the person or persons involved in other organizations to determine their knowledge, possession and action to date on the matter.**

An assumption here is that many projects will involve people and activities in both the initiating organization and other organizations that might or will play a role in the project if it is carried out to its logical conclusion. At this step you will move outside your organization to check with others in other organizations to determine their actions (if any), their knowledge (did they read the material sent to them?), the aspects of the project that are in their possession currently and their interest in seeing the project brought to a conclusion.

3. **Determination of what actions should be taken next on the basis of the outcome of #1 and #2 above. This is the setting of priorities within the larger goal of accomplishing the project.**

Now you determine where you are. What has happened and what problems and opportunities do the actions to date create? What changes in plans from the original are suggested? What modifications will you then make? Once any modifications are made, they need to be thought through and communicated. What now is priority #1? What priorities follow that? To whom should each of these priorities be assigned? What resources does the person responsible need? What time should be allowed for completion of the various priorities? Should some priorities be worked on simultaneously and others only in sequence?

4. **Communication with others about these priorities.**

Who needs to be communicated with at this point in the process including any approvals needed for proceeding? Who should do the communicating and by what means? Is it an issue of granting approval or extending information? If communicating information only, it is often best to communicate by fax or e-mail if the information is not lengthy. However, beware of the tendency to send information in this fashion when part of your motive is to avoid any possible confrontation with another person or group. If that face-to-face contact is essential to the project or to you personally or professionally, tackle it now. Arrange the face-to-face meeting or, if that is not practical, the voice-to-voice contact. Remember, your goal is to complete what you set out to do, not just to make life easier for yourself at the moment. Most confrontations don't turn out to be as bad as our minds conjure up that they might be. Communicate, communicate, communicate. If there is any doubt about the need to communicate, there is a need to communicate.

5. **Tackling priority #1—what is it, who needs to be involved, what action should be taken and in what priority?**

If the project has a good chance of success, the goal was clearly spelled out at the beginning. If it was not clearly stated then, do it now. A poorly conceived goal has virtually no chance of success.

The process of preparing a written statement of the goal will also have the impact of clarifying your personal thoughts. The clearer the goal, the less effort it will take to reach it. A clear goal allows you to go to an address rather than a neighborhood or a city.

Now that the goal is very clear, what needs to be done at this stage of its history? Who should do it and how urgent is its completion?

"Do something" is usually better than to do nothing but "do something" is insufficiently descriptive. Unless you are in an emergency situation, take the time to be specific about what should be done now. Based upon what that is, decide who should do it and on what timetable.

Don't forget the timing. A job done very well but late might be worthless or damaging. People often work on their own timetables unless it is made very clear that the project has a timetable. Make it clear.

6. **Seeing that priority #1 is done—accomplished with excellence on a timely basis.**

    Make sure the person knows both the task expected and the timetable expected. Then set up procedures by which that person's progress will be monitored. You do not want to find out too late that the person dropped the ball, is doing the task incorrectly or is doing more harm than good. Anything worth doing is an act that is worth supervising (monitoring).

    The best way to ensure excellence in getting something done is to set up standards and procedures at the outset of a project. What will define excellence? What procedures will keep the project on a track of excellence? These need not be long in detail, but they need to be explicit enough to keep the person responsible for the project mindful of the excellence that is to be attained.

Whatever we do, it is worth doing well. We should never judge ourselves or others on the basis of how much we have done. Rather, the criteria should be how much we did well.

7. **Repeat the process with the remaining priorities.**

The six steps above take care of the first priority. Other priorities might be even more important but need to be done on a different schedule and thus have a different priority. The interior decorating in a new house is very important. But it is not a priority until the house has been built.

What is the next priority? Treat it with the same care that you did the first priority. Do it well and do it on time.

8. **Monitor the overall process to correct any activity that gets out of sync with the other actions and take corrective action as required.**

Effective management requires effective monitoring. Monitoring does not mean interference; it means knowing what is going on at all times including how the project measures against both quality criteria and timeliness criteria. The person who notices that no one cares enough about his or her work to observe it or ask questions about it is not likely to do the best work he or she is capable of doing. You can't give an "atta boy" for work you know nothing about. As Ken Blanchard has said in *The One Minute Manager*, "catch people doing something right."[1]

It is currently fashionable to have much of the supervision done by teams in which each person is responsible to every other member of the team for achieving excellence and timeliness. Whether you use this method or more traditional management, it is essential that there be a quality control monitoring of every action and process in an organization.

What if the monitoring reveals a problem? Then what? You must have the courage to correct what the problem seems to be. Effective managing involves using corrective procedures as well as developing broad new plans. Sometimes management surgery is needed. Christian managers need to act sensitively and with concern for each individual employee while taking the action that is overall the best for the organization.

9. **Ensure that there is closure. Either the project is brought to a successful conclusion or it is clearly dropped—no project is left active with no action.**

Loose ends tend to unravel. In terms of something you are trying to complete, a loose end is a detail left unattended. Something that is a minor detail to you might be a major factor to someone else. Checklists are often very helpful in ensuring that details as well as major responsibilities are not overlooked. Do what works for you, but be sure to do it.

I recently had the experience of working on a major project over a period of two years. The project was concluded according to a handshake, but the written document was very elusive and never came about. In fact, the handshake was not as conclusive as it appeared. The fact that one thing after another kept one of the participants in the project from completing his part of the written report was an indication that we had a loose end that had the potential of unraveling all the work of the past two years. Only through continually keeping after that loose end did the project ever get concluded.

10. **Report on the outcome of the project to all those with an interest in knowing about it.**

If the project involved a considerable expenditure of energy to get it completed, we can be sure that there will be various persons and groups very interested in the outcome. To stop when we know what we have been wanting to know is to be self-centered. The project will not have its proper effect until everyone who has a need to know has received some communication about the consummation of the project with details as they relate to that person or group. This, too, needs to be timely. Most efforts at communication require the same energy whether they are done on a timely basis or not. Procrastination actually requires energy because the disorganization, reminders and lack of peace of mind all require energy. If it should be communicated now, do it now. Then turn your energies to your next project.

How Are Strategies Written?

First of all, strategies might be categorized. Some of the categories for a major goal (such as starting a business in the case study above) could be as follows:

1. Are there subgoals? What are they? Possibly each should have written strategies.

2. What are the people implications? What others will be needed in the accomplishment of this goal? How will I enlist their support? Are there some alternatives?

3. What are the financial implications? If my goal is to move into a larger and nicer house within the next two years, there are financial implications. A strategy for saving, a strategy for maximizing current assets (such as my current house) so as to have the most assets possible when the time comes, a strategy for finding other resources such as cashing in stocks or selling other things I own and a strategy for getting the down payment I can afford when the time comes are all strategies that I should consider. Then I need to put them into

writing today so that the goal has a greater chance of being realized when two years from now is here.

4. What are the physical limitations? If the goal is to do something that I cannot physically do now and see no way of being able to do then, this is an absolute reality check that I need to take another look at the goal. Physical demands go beyond us personally. Examine the example above of buying a house. What are the physical limitations there? If a member of the family is physically unable to climb stairs, then the acquisition of a house that has no stairs is a necessary requisite to meet this very real physical limitation.

5. What are the psychological factors involved both as incentives and restraints? What will even the statement of the goal do to how I feel, how others feel? What would happen if the goal were to be realized?

6. What is the impact upon the world around me? What about its influence upon the larger surroundings? What are the ethical implications in my goal?

7. What is God's will in this? Is the statement of the goal pleasing to God? What if I accomplish this goal? How will God react to it? Am I ready for this reaction? Is it something for which I have been longing?

Second, a strategy is written as an action item. Something happens as the result of a strategy being successfully carried out. Action is the key word here.

When you write a strategy, keep in mind the goal and what action you are spelling out in that strategy. If your goal is to learn how to play the piano, a strategy might be to find a piano teacher. The action here is find. Another strategy might be to locate a piano on which to practice. The action here is locate. Think of your goal and think of the actions needed to make the goal a reality.

Developing Strategies For Every Prioritized Goal

Many goals, many priorities and many strategies. How do we keep them organized so that we are not tripping over our own efforts? Here are some suggestions:

1. Write down your goals, priorities and strategies.

2. Keep them no more complex than they need to be. Write in standard English.

3. Organize all of this so they are easily accessible. A computer does this well.

4. Check off or mark goals that have been achieved. In this way you see progress.

5. Keep goals and their priorities and strategies together.

6. Keep the information with you all the time. Have a printout of the goals, in particular, where you will see them throughout the day.

7. Let others around you know of your goals. They might be of some help from time to time.

8. Pray about your goals, priorities and strategies. Seek God's will in all that you do.

9. Keep focused on your goals. It is easy to get involved in the goals of others. Sometimes you need to help others with their goals but not every minute of every day. Remember, you can help others best when your own goals are being met.

10. Be of courage. Act out your commitment. If it is the right thing to do, start acting on it right now.

Keeping Strategies Vibrant

If our strategies are not vibrant, we will not accomplish our goals. Life is most satisfying when we see our goals reach fruition.

What does it mean for a strategy to be vibrant? Vibrancy relates to being active, appropriate, exciting, positive, fun, attractive and likely to produce results. A strategy with these characteristics is one which will help us to achieve our goals, our desired results.

Goals are not normally set without the hope of completing them. But goals are seldom accomplished unless the primary person responsible for that goal sets priorities and strategies for the accomplishment of that goal. Strategies remain vibrant through constant attention, through being utilized as intended to reach the goal. Review your strategies from time to time to ensure that they remain appropriate to the goal. Don't be afraid to change a strategy; at the same time, do not change a strategy simply because it appears that it is not working. Make your strategies work for you.

Endnote

[1]Kenneth Blanchard and Spencer Johnson, *The One Minute Manager* (New York, NY: Berkley Books, 1983), p. 40.

Chapter Nine

Coping With A Complex, Stress-Filled And Self-Centered World

And we know that in all things God works for the good of those who love him, who have been called according to his purpose. — Romans 8:28

The Concept of Principles and Preferences

Each of us confuses principles with preferences. The more a person feels he or she lives by principles, the more this confusion is likely to occur. Both start with the letter "p" which might contribute to the confusion some people have. Let's look at the fundamental differences between a principle and a preference.

Principles

Certain characteristics are common to all principles. Principles:

- endure over time.
- change little amidst changing circumstances.
- can be applied to different situations.
- can be applied by different people.
- can be simply stated.
- should be used as a guide.
- state that under certain circumstances, A or B will happen.
- cross languages and cultures.
- must be learned for success where it applies.
- are not equal in breadth but all have broad application.
- are followed by both experts and novices.
- assume a set of circumstances; when those circumstances change, a different principle will apply.
- will, in a few cases, be outmoded because the circumstances upon which they were based will no longer exist.
- are not equal in importance but the most important principles will never be outmoded.
- are handy guides to doing things right; they are learned and practiced by those who wish to succeed.
- are generally ethical but unethical people have principles for their survival as well.
- have unique applications for Christians; Christians need to learn and practice these.

Some principles apply to life in general, others apply to how to manage an organization while others are specific to managing an oil well. In each case, you need to learn these principles and apply them if you are involved in that activity. Because all of us are involved in life in general, we must learn these. Not many of us are involved in oil well management. Figure out what you are involved in and determine what the principles are that apply to those activities.

Robert Fulgram in his book, *All I Really Need to Know I Learned in Kindergarten*, wrote about some of the principles he had observed that are learned in kindergarten.[1] Some are pretty simple, like "Wash your hands before you eat." However, many principles are amazingly simple. Many if not most of the principles we need to learn about life are taught to us early. As a young boy I was taught the principles:

"Never hit a girl."
"Always tell the truth."
"Say your prayers before you eat."
"Treat others the way you want to be treated."
"Be fair."
"Wash your hands before you eat."
"Open the door for a girl or lady."
"Never swear or use bad language."

There were many others. Women will recall other principles that uniquely apply to them and that they learned as they were growing up. As adults we assume that other adults have been taught the principles we know and that they will practice them. We are sometimes disappointed. But principles like these guide how persons interact with each other every day. The principles I learned as a boy still guide me today. I apply them in a little different way because my circumstances have changed, but the basic principles remain the same.

We get careless about the practice of some of these principles. As time is short or because we think that the principle is just for children, we start to skip some of the principles. One of these is the one about washing your hands before you eat. However, a recent medical study pointed out that a breakout of disease in a school could have been avoided or stopped if everyone had simply washed their hands thoroughly before eating.

As we move to such areas as managing a small business or managing a segment of a large corporation, there are other principles that apply in addition to the basic ones like those above that have universal application. One of the times that I taught a college course in Principles of Management I required each student during the semester to record every management principle they encountered either in class, in the text or in their daily experiences. The students were surprised at the number and diversity of the principles that they found.

The point behind learning principles is that wisdom has produced them for us. We cannot possibly as individuals discover every principle on our own. We profit by learning from others. We gain this through education and experience. Be observant of the principles which apply to your life and to your work. Record some of them as you go along and you will find these principles valuable to observe as your life progresses.

Preferences

Now let's look at preferences. Preferences:

- are unique to the individual expressing them.
- are often mistakenly thought of as principles by an individual who holds this preference so intensely.
- express how each of us can add diversity to our culture in both positive and negative ways.
- can be intensely held.
- can be based upon bias, prejudice and inadequate observation; such preferences need to be changed by the individual through goal setting.
- are often based upon what we are taught early in life.
- are often based upon a specific set of circumstances we have encountered.
- are not necessarily good for us even though we think they are.
- are often based upon rationalization.
- can be strongly linked to principles in a very effective manner by using preferences where the principles do not apply.
- are the way we express our creativity.
- are the way we express our personalities.
- allow us to set ourselves apart from others in both good and bad ways.

- are sometimes disguised as principles in public rhetoric by politicians attempting to gain our support for their preferences.
- should be expressed by every individual.
- should never be confused with a principle by anyone.
- add uniqueness, beauty and enjoyment to life when appropriately applied.

Each of us has many preferences. We express our preferences in what we wear, how we do our hair (if we have any — my choices are quite limited there due to natural causes), what we choose to eat, how we fix what we eat, the type of car we choose to drive, how we drive that car. Based upon our preferences we make choices every minute we are awake of every day. Not all of our choices are good choices. We sometimes say or do things that are not good and that are not consistent with our value systems. But behavior is a new page every day, and we have the opportunity to make new choices based upon our preferences every day and we do.

Principles and preferences are both important positive elements in our lives. **The point here is that we should never confuse the two.** Both need to be implemented but preferences should always be exercised within the framework of the principles that apply. In other words, when the two are in conflict, the principle should rule. Be sure you are applying the right principle to the situation, and be sure that your motives do not include trying to manipulate or rationalize a situation to make it appear that some principle applies to that specific situation when it does not. Not all situations in life are governed by a principle. We do not have preferences about all things either, although some people have preferences (opinions) about almost everything.

Principles and Preferences Relationship

When you make a decision based upon a preference, be sure you are aware of any principle that applies to the situation. Then examine your preference to ensure that it is not based upon bias or prejudice and that it is really your preference. Sometimes we state preferences because we think that is what others want to hear or what will boost our ego. When we lie to ourselves like that, we end up in situations where we don't want to be. **Think** about your preference in a given situation before expressing it to others or making a decision based upon your preferences.

Principles, Preferences And Christian Faith

How do principles and preferences relate to your Christian faith? Your Christian faith should be the source of the major principles guiding your life. A number of separate principles will come from your Christian faith to guide your relationships with others (see Chapter Ten for more on relationships), your self-concept, your relationship with God, your outlook on life and your attitude toward work. **Your Christian faith defines the person you are by the principles within Christianity that you choose to direct your life.**

Our Stress-filled Culture

People in some cultures experience more stress than others. People in some cultures are more productive than others. Cultures differ in other important ways. Some of the characteristics of our culture are:

- to conform. Unless we are "stars" in some way, we are pressured to be like others.
- to be successful. As opposed to excellence.
- to be independent. We are democratic in spirit, yet mostly in private (voting) or in giving opinions, rather than in our behavior (where we tend to conform).
- to handle stress. We are looked down upon when stress gets the best of us.
- to display our status. We display our status in such visible things as houses, cars and clothes.

- to seek comfort, less work. We emphasize labor-saving devices.
- to be creative. We give some credit to creative people as long as their creativity falls within societal norms.
- to be religious. We claim membership in churches but do not mention that we do not attend. We are not encouraged to be Christlike except by the Christian community.
- to impose pressure and stress on ourselves. We tend to strongly criticize ourselves.
- to be hard working, productive. This is related to being successful.

We discover the pressures of a culture by noting what the media portrays as good and what it portrays as bad. Mother Teresa of Calcutta was good; a criminal is bad. There are some false messages that come from the media because of its liberal leanings (the press is generally more of an advocate for change in our society than the general population is).

What Stress Is

Stress is pressure. Sometimes we feel stress because we do not understand the problem and have no clear solutions. Stress weighs upon all of us, but it weighs more heavily upon some than others. Not all stress is bad. There is much in the medical press about good stress. We all need some pressure upon us to keep us going.

Cause of Stress

Some stress is culture induced (as, for example, our culture puts pressure upon us to conform in type of dress), but much of the pressure of stress comes from within ourselves and from those immediately around us including our families and friends.

It might be logical to think that family and friends would not do that to us. They should be the ones to nourish and support us. For the most part they do. But at the same time our spouses, parents, children and friends all see the world in a different way than we see the world. Each of us lives according to a unique set of principles, and we all have different preferences (some of them self-serving). When our preferences and those of a family member or friend are in conflict, stress occurs. For some people this becomes very stressful. For Christians, this should be less stressful because of our love of God and all of His creation. It is important that Christians love one another rather than tear one another down, but this does not always occur particularly when emotions are running high. This may well be why God created parents in twos; when one is emotionally expressive, the other can be the moderating influence.

Probably the greatest source of stress is from within ourselves. We set standards for ourselves and are very critical when we do not meet those standards. I have the bad habit of setting something down without realizing what I have done. Then later I cannot find that item. I am upset with myself because the standard I have set for myself is that I should never lose anything and that I should always know where things are.

A Healthy Self-Respect

While others might be critical of us, it is essential that we have a healthy respect for ourselves. We cannot let the criticisms of others and from within ourselves contribute to the conclusion that we are not worthy individuals. We are created by God. As the bumper sticker says, "God didn't create any junk." While this topic can be the focus of a whole book (see the bibliography at the end of the book), we can say briefly here that there are several principles you should observe:

- You must respect yourself as a creation of God. To do any less is to criticize God.

- You must be in control of your own adult life. You must not let others control (influence, define) your actions and thoughts to the point that you cannot assume responsibility for who you are. The New Testament does not talk about controlling others. The New Testament talks to and about each of us as individuals. This is not to be interpreted that you are exempt from the controls of our society. There are rules which all of us must observe in order to live in an orderly world.

- You must love and respect others as fellow creatures of God. In doing so you will help them to reach toward their full potential, to use their abilities, talents, spiritual gifts and skills.

- God must be the primary focus of your life. Your principles are based upon the quality of this focus All behavior must be measured against God's standards.

Success and Excellence

As noted in the stress list above, there is pressure in our society to be successful with success being defined in terms of status, power and worldly possessions. This is a particular challenge for the Christian who is taught to avoid worshiping the things of this world. Yet Jesus never said that a rich man cannot enter heaven; He just said it would be very difficult. "Again I tell you, it is easier for a camel to go through the eye of a needle than for a rich man to enter the kingdom of God" (Matthew 19:24). This is not because of the wealth itself but because of what wealth can do to the mind of an individual such as the "rich, young ruler."

> Now a man came up to Jesus and asked, "Teacher, what good thing must I do to get eternal life?" "Why do you ask me about what is good?" Jesus replied. "There is only One who is good. If you want to enter life, obey the commandments." "Which ones?" the man inquired. Jesus replied, "'Do not murder, do not commit adultery, do not steal, do not give false testimony, honor your father and mother,' and 'love your neighbor as yourself.'" "All these I have kept," the young man said. "What do I still lack?"

> Jesus answered, "If you want to be perfect, go, sell your possessions and give to the poor, and you will have treasure in heaven. Then come, follow me." When the young man heard this, he went away sad, because he had great wealth (Matthew 19:16-22).

Thus the Christian can obtain earthly possessions as long as the possessions do not come to be the center of the person's life instead of God.

The Christian should be encouraged toward excellence instead of success as defined by this world. See the book by Jon Johnston, *Christian Excellence* (Second Edition), in the bibliography. Excellence means doing the best you can do in whatever you do. Some of the results of excellence are the same as the results of success. Excellence in what you do might produce earthly possessions. But the possessions are not the goal of excellence. The goal of excellence is to use the talents, abilities, spiritual gifts and skills we have to do the very best we are capable of doing in whatever part of God's Kingdom that we make our contributions.

Retirement

Note here that the Bible does not talk about retirement. A recent article in *Christian Standard* suggests that adults, when they reach retirement age, are not only influential but also have great physical energy. This group has marvelous potential to contribute to society.[2] An earlier article in the same magazine recounted how a newly retired Frigidaire foreman in Ohio with no training as a minister or a social worker began a nursing home ministry that lasted for twenty-two years. His motivation gave him the persistence and creativity to develop new abilities and skills for a second career. He continued his work as long as he had physical strength.[3] If retirement means only that you no longer go to the job you went to for many years because you are at an age or state of physical health that you can no longer do that job, that is one thing. But the Bible does not condone idleness even if a person is not working for a living.

There are so many things people without a job but with varying degrees of good health can do to make this a better world. If this category fits you, work on relieving stress in the lives of others through the use of your talents, spiritual gifts, abilities and skills. Life will be more rewarding and you are likely to live longer.

Stress and Christianity

Christians are both admired and scorned by our society. We are admired for the most part as moral people. We are criticized as hypocrites who do not live the religion they espouse. Although Christians are less than a majority in the world, a majority of people in the United States claim to be Christians. If our faith is to be vibrant, we must find ways to combat the sources of stress that society hands us. Further, we must certainly find ways to overcome the sources of stress that come from within ourselves. Stress is in conflict with our faith. We must ensure that our Christian faith is paramount, that the strength that comes from it will help us to address the challenges of stress.

Handling Chaos, Complexity and Adversity

Chaos

A best-selling book by Tom Peters is entitled *Thriving On Chaos: A Handbook For A Management Revolution.*[4] This and similar books and teachings break away from the tradition that the most organized is always the best because it then means that goals are clear, resources are lined up, management is in place and all other factors for organizational success are present. Why then an emphasis on chaos? A reading of Peters will demonstrate that he is not trying to create chaos, but he is recognizing that it is part of our culture today and that part of success today is understanding how to take advantage of this chaos. How does chaos come about?

Chaos can come as a result of considerable change and flexibility that will disrupt traditional goals, strategies and other ways of doing things. In a time of chaos, the rules for success change roughly in proportion to the amount of chaos. This is true for individuals as well as for organizations. We live in a period of chaos, change, innovation and flexibility. We can have feelings of being happy, angry or sad about it but that will not change the fact. What does this mean for Christians who want to manage themselves effectively?

It will mean taking advantage of these changes in society instead of letting the changes destroy your opportunities and current successes. In order to take advantage of this situation, you and I must have some awareness of the change that affects our particular situations. This requires us to be learning persons, to read, to listen, to discuss and otherwise learn from others about what is happening in the world closest to us. Do not depend upon others to educate you. It is your own responsibility to inform yourself, to ferret out information, to assimilate that information, to analyze it and to use it in a way that is helpful to you. Don't let the change in the world pass you by and leave you obsolete. This must be a major part of the challenge you understand and act upon each day.

To deal with chaos, we try to bring some order to it. Apparent chaos might just have a smoke screen in front of it that catches the eyes of everyone. If we can get past the smoke screen, we might expedite the process of understanding the situation. Even if the situation is clearly chaotic, some analysis often helps to restore perspective. What created the chaos? What do we know about the situation? What timing factors are involved (is it explosive, will it change very soon)? How might we relate to it from our experience and connections? What would we want to get from the situation, if anything? Is it worth our while to become involved in the situation? Could we help society by being involved?

Now that we have discussed the need to cope with change and even chaos, how do we take advantage of it? Much of it is through an inquiring approach to the world around us, constantly looking for an opportunity, for an advantage. A number of periodicals cater to this form of thinking. The magazine *Entrepreneur* is written for the person who takes ideas and turns them into products and services and thus profit. *Success* magazine focuses upon helping us as readers to understand that yes, we can succeed, even in spite of considerable difficulty if we really put our minds to it. Success, the reader comes to understand, is not dependent upon having a lot of money, past success, experience or position. It does depend upon having a good idea and the willingness to do whatever it takes to make the idea work. Of course, not all ideas do work but a surprising number become successful when the basic ingredients for success are present. Success, however, is usually complex.

Complexity

Let's look at the issue of complexity. Complexity suggests many parts in relationship with each other. It further suggests something that is not easy to understand. Complexity is much like chaos. Both make a situation difficult to understand and require considerable effort in order to determine how to act when faced with these situations. Complexity can be very structured as in a complex chemical formula, or complexity can be laced with chaos as in the case of determining the causes of crimes in a city. How we approach complexity depends upon the extent to which it is related to chaos.

Dealing with complexity requires knowledge and analytical ability in order to perceive what needs to be known and then what to do about it. Dealing with chaos draws heavily upon intuition to figure out what is happening and then what to do about it. Complex chaos, as in the crime illustration above, requires both sets of tools in order to be successful.

Adversity

The world we live in is certainly complex. It is complicated by being partially chaotic. If that were not enough, there is also the issue of adversity by which individuals and/or groups are pitted against one another. Or in another manifestation of adversity we find ourselves in a difficult set of circumstances. Charles Stanley has written a book, *How To Handle Adversity,* in which he talks about the sources of adversity. Stanley comments that God is the source of some adversity. Other adversity can come from within ourselves. Other people or situations are other causes.[5] But the important issue is not so much who or what caused the adversity as it is what to do when we find ourselves in adversity. The situation surrounding the death of Lazarus is an example of adversity caused by a situation but which extends to human relations.[6]

In the situations of adversity that I have faced, I have noticed that situations which involve me as an individual are the most difficult situations of adversity to face and to solve. If I remain detached from a situation in which I am counseling two individuals about a disagreement, being a part of the solution seems much easier. Why is this so? In part it is because it is difficult for us to analyze, to be rational about adversity which involves us personally. The anxiety caused by the adversity tends to keep us from being able to help bring about the solution.

Adversity, like chaos, needs some fact-finding and analysis at the outset. This might not do away with the adversity (such as in the death of a friend) but might help us deal with the effects of the adversity.

Stanley points out in the situation with Lazarus that Jesus did not panic in the face of adversity. Jesus even let the situation become worse. Likewise, each of us needs to face adversity as calmly and rationally as possible. This is a time when Christian fellowship can be important to each of us. We need to work to keep the adversity in perspective. Foolish actions sometimes are precipitated by adversity—situations in which we either become extremely frustrated or just give up (the basis for many suicides). At the same time there is a natural process of grieving the loss of a loved one (see the works of Joseph Bayly[7]) or recovering from other situations. We need to recognize this process and let it run its course while refraining from doing anything we will regret later.

As each us of faces chaos, complexity and even adversity, we must be mindful of the Romans 8 passage quoted at the beginning of this chapter. Although it might be difficult for us to understand why God would either cause or let happen a number of situations on earth, we are comforted by knowing that the things that we would prefer to avoid are part of a larger plan that God has for those who love Him. It might take years for the good to be evident. It could even be that the good will never be apparent to us during our lifetimes. He does not guarantee that He will reveal the reason. He only guarantees that it will work together for good. Thus, we must trust and not let our faith be negatively affected in the long run by situations of adversity that we are in now or have experienced previously.

Checking Out Our Own Mental Health

Physical Health

What is written in this book assumes that you are physically and psychologically able to do what you are encouraged to do. Virtually all of us have some physical limitations so we are not just addressing those who enjoy perfect health. The key to defining physical limitations in physical health is in what it really keeps you from doing. If you stop doing something because it makes you perspire or because it takes more effort than it used to or because there is some minor pain connected with it, then you are still talking about personal choice rather than limitation. It is very true that as we get older we acquire more physical limitations. What I am suggesting is that you refuse to let those physical limitations pose a greater limitation on you than is necessary within the recommendation of your physician.

One of the saddest pictures of people as they grow older is that they reach a certain age and give up. Or they give up when they face their first physical limitation, such as in how far they can walk. We should never attempt to act against a physician's recommendation, but we need to remember that the body will atrophy faster when it is not used. You are encouraged to do everything you want to do that your body will reasonably permit without endangering yourself physically.

My mother, as I write this, is ninety-four and my father is ninety-six. He still drives a car (he bought a new car when he was ninety) almost every day and they go for short trips. They have been married seventy-two years and live in their own house. Mother has to use a walker because she is unsteady on her feet. Father reads quite a bit, and I take him books and magazines when I am able to be there for a visit. They attend church, weather and health permitting. To be sure, they are fortunate in their good health. My point is that they will keep themselves going longer because they do interesting things to keep their minds active, read often and visit with others when they have the opportunity. They enjoy life. They have not given up. You are encouraged to enjoy life regardless of your age as well.

Psychological Health

Some psychological problems humans face are beyond their own control. Other conditions are brought on by circumstances, some of which are controlled by the individual. An active mind with a series of positive experiences seems to be the only antidote to mental illness.

Most of us have some psychological limitations. I have claustrophobia, the fear of closed-in spaces. I also have acrophobia, the fear of heights. This one I am gradually overcoming, but it is real nonetheless. What psychological limitations do you face? How have they affected your ability to work and to relate on a positive basis with other people? If your problems have had no effect that you are aware of, you are fortunate.

To help you evaluate how others see you, you might want to take the following short test to question the perception others have of you to see if there might be some other personal aspect that might need attention physically or psychologically:

1. Am I still tired during the day after a normal night's sleep?
2. Am I angry or very discouraged more than 5 percent of the time?
3. To what extent am I in good health?
4. Do I have habits that work against good health, such as overeating, smoking, alcohol, stress, anger, lack of sleep, other)?
5. To what extent do I feel: (5 is high)

a. Persecuted	1	2	3	4	5
b. Loved	1	2	3	4	5
c. Appreciated	1	2	3	4	5
d. Hated	1	2	3	4	5
e. Respected	1	2	3	4	5
f. Ignored	1	2	3	4	5
g. Admired	1	2	3	4	5
h. Avoided	1	2	3	4	5

6. To what extent do I: (5 is high)

a. Appreciate others	1	2	3	4	5
b. Love others	1	2	3	4	5
c. Enjoy being around others	1	2	3	4	5
d. Think positively	1	2	3	4	5
e. Respect others	1	2	3	4	5
f. Like others	1	2	3	4	5
g. Enjoy being with other people	1	2	3	4	5
h. Admire others	1	2	3	4	5
i. Have a "servant's heart"	1	2	3	4	5
j. Respect my elders	1	2	3	4	5
k. Serve as a role model for youth	1	2	3	4	5
l. Like myself	1	2	3	4	5
m. Live a life of integrity	1	2	3	4	5
n. Listen well to others	1	2	3	4	5
o. Express myself clearly	1	2	3	4	5
p. Think others know me as a Christian	1	2	3	4	5

q.	Enjoy life	1	2	3	4	5
r.	Pray regularly	1	2	3	4	5
s.	Have goals upon which I act	1	2	3	4	5

Add up your scores from question 6b, c, e, g, and i. If you have a score of 25 you have probably been too optimistic. A healthy score would be 17-24. Then add up your scores on 6a, d, f, and h. A healthy score would be 4 to 7. If your scores were outside of what is suggested as a healthy score, look carefully at the specific items which caused your score to be outside the suggested range. Remember that these scores represent how others see you, not what you really are.

After you have honestly answered the above questions about yourself, think about each item—particularly those with a score of 1, 2, 4 or 5. What does this say about you? Is any action by you suggested?

Whatever the above indicates to you, act now on any possible problem area so that any limitation upon your life from that problem area might be confronted.

What We Do/What We Permit/What We Oppose

Each of us has a set of values upon which we base our behavior every hour of the day. We do certain things because we feel they are right, and we avoid other things because we feel they are wrong. These are our convictions. They are our decisions based upon our understandings (our value systems) of what is right and wrong.

But not all decisions we make are based upon a sense of right and wrong. In fact, most of them aren't. This would include the decision to order ravioli instead of soup and salad in a restaurant, the decision to wear the clothes we picked out this morning, the decision of how much of the newspaper to read, the decision to mow the yard today instead of tomorrow. These all assume, of course, that there is no hidden motive or a values issue behind those decisions. I do not mow grass on Sunday as a values decision, but whether I do it on Thursday or

Friday or Monday is not a values decision. These are decisions of convenience and personal preference.

Often the mundane decisions we make have a values implication. If I cut the grass on Friday after promising my wife I would do it on Thursday, then values become involved. If I don't cut it at all for some time, I might be making a values decision because such a decision might offend my neighbor whose grass is cut more often. So there is no really clean separation between decisions that have values built into them and those that don't.

Each of the major values decisions we make falls into one of three categories. There are those we make positively because we believe it is the right thing to do (consistent with our values system). Then there are those decisions we make negatively because our values tell us to be opposed to it. But there are also many decisions we make by default on issues where we decide to take no action. This could be because we have no position on a certain issue (our values do not address it). Or it could be that our values do address the issue, but we lack the courage to take the action we should be taking. In the latter case we have a values problem because we lack sufficient courage to act.

There is a major difference between courage and foolishness. Some people will do things like going off a bungee jump that, in my opinion, is not courage but foolishness. Remember, though, I am afraid of heights. You show courage when you do something your values tell you to do but either societal pressure or physical pain or another factor makes the accomplishment of it difficult. Courage is what we saw in the 1996 Summer Olympics when Kerri Strug went on with her performance when she was obviously in pain. Her focus was so good that she came back and won the Gold Medal for the U. S. women's gymnastics team. She became the grand marshal of the Fiesta Bowl Parade in recognition of her courage. In another case, President Harry Truman exhibited great courage when he authorized the bombing of Japan in order to expedite the ending of World War II. Courage means there is some risk involved to the individual or to someone or something they represent, but they proceed with the action anyway because they are convinced that it is the right thing to do. Criminals have no courage to do the right thing. Some of us are reluctant to show our courage. Think about the courage you have. What would you be willing to risk in order to stand up for what you believe is right?

Ego and Self-centeredness

Ego relates to believing in ourselves. In order to make it through each day, we must possess healthy egos. We must believe that we have the ability to do what we need to do. We need to believe that we are persons created by God with spiritual gifts and talents that can help make this a better world.

Our problem comes when the ego becomes too large, when we begin to think only of what is good for ourselves. It is true that in order to help others, we must first take care of ourselves— we must eat, sleep and care for our health. Ego is becoming too large when our part of any conversation emphasizes what we have done, what we think or what we will do with little emphasis upon others in the conversation. It is OK to talk about yourself at times; the problem comes in the balance of the conversation. How much of what you say is designed to impress others with who you are, what you think and what you know?

A person who is mature and self-assured will tend to carry on a conversation with an individual by asking them questions about themselves. An occasional comment about self is appropriate. It is better for someone to ask about your status, your opinion or your knowledge than to force it upon others. They will get more from the discussion and will get more enjoyment out of talking with you.

Communicating Effectively

There are times when we have thought about something long enough that we think that we have communicated the whole process to others. We tend to think that they know what we know about our thoughts. In fact, in such an instance we have not communicated effectively. There are times as well when we do not listen effectively because we think we know already what the person is about to say. When we do that, we are not communicating effectively. When someone else knows something that we need to know and does not tell us but thinks he or she already has, there is a communication problem.

A high proportion of the human interaction problems (see Chapter Ten) that we encounter are either caused by or made worse by communication problems. If you know that you and another person need to talk about something, you should never use the excuse that initiating the conversation is the responsibility of the other person. By doing that you are saying that catching that person failing to do something is more important than having the needed conversation. The person who takes the initiative in communicating always has the advantage of determining when, under what circumstances and with what preparation the conversation takes place.

Your personal life and professional career are dependent upon your ability to communicate effectively. Regardless of whether it is receiving or sending communication, look upon it as your responsibility for seeing that it happens effectively.

Coping Through a Rational, Personal Plan

Life is a challenge. There will be days when you feel it is more of a challenge than you are able to meet. Nonetheless, God created us with the ability, I am convinced, to stand up to anything that life hands to us. We need not face the challenges alone. God is with us. Prayer and Bible study will help us be closer to God and thus feel His strength in all that challenges us. Second, we have Christian friends. If you are a Christian without friends, start hanging out in churches that have vibrant programs. You will find friends. Rely on them as a source of strength.

God's intention is that you will be able to address your problems and challenges with the help of God and your Christian friends. You will be helped in this by having a rational, personal plan which is centered on your goals for the future. In earlier chapters we talked about goals, about setting priorities among those goals and, finally, creating strategies for the accomplishment of each of those goals. By setting goals, priorities and strategies you are assuming responsibility for your life. Do it now and start enjoying the fruits of your planning.

Endnotes

[1]Robert Fulgram, *All I Really Need To Know I Learned In Kindergarten* (New York, NY: Ivy Books, 1993).

[2]Win Arn and Charles Arn, "A New Paradigm for Ministry: Middle Adults," *Christian Standard* (September 22, 1996), pp. 7-8.

[3]Paul A. Blaum, "Henry Whitehair: In Memoriam," *Christian Standard* (October 29, 1995), pp. 12-13.

[4]Tom Peters, *Thriving On Chaos: A Handbook For A Management Revolution* (New York, NY: Alfred A. Knopf, 1988).

[5]Charles Stanley, *How To Handle Adversity* (Nashville, TN: Thomas Nelson Publishers, 1989), pp. 11-20.

[6]"Lord, if you had been here, my brother would not have died" (John 11:21, 31).

[7]Joseph Bayly, *The Last Thing We Talk About: Help And Hope For Those Who Grieve* (Elgin, IL: Chariot Family Publishers, 1992); Also, by the same author, *Out Of My Mind: The Best Of Joe Bayly* (Grand Rapids, MI: Zondervan Publishing House, 1993).

Chapter Ten

Extending The Self To Others: Showing Compassion

Try not to become a man of success but rather a man of value. —
Albert Einstein

God uses different people with different personalities in different ways to build His church. Determined Paul; inspiring Peter; sensitive John; conscientious James; different as they were, all fulfilled a unique mission in serving our Lord Jesus Christ. — Ken Voges and Ron Braund

The opportunities to show compassion for others are always with us; it is the getting to a concern for others rather than self that is difficult. — Kenneth W. Oosting

t is difficult for the human individual to get beyond the self. We are always with ourselves; this is the only nonchanging part of our environments. Other people, places and things constantly change in our lives. But the self is always there. Now self will itself undergo change, but it is still self. It is always you or I.

How we feel about ourselves is very important to our approach to the rest of the world. If we don't like ourselves, it is likely that we will not like anything else (persons included). If we are enjoying life to the fullest, others around us will not only notice, but they will be affected by it as well. The way we treat others and affect them in positive ways is closely linked to our capacity to enjoy life. Are you a positive force in the lives of others?

Probably most of us at one time or another in our lives give some thought to the kind of persons we would like to be (and hopefully some thought to the kind of persons we really are). When we identify the areas of differences between the persons we would like to be and the persons we actually are, we are able to think more clearly about what we should do about the differences.

Our Heroes

When we do this we think of our heroes. For most of us, our real heroes are not people widely known or who are in the news. They are people we have known or currently know who present a model for us in some area of our lives. At times we might have a model we use for most areas of our lives. Think about those who might be models in your life.

As I think of such role models for me, I think of Marvin Johnson. Marvin Johnson, or Mr. Johnson as I thought of him, was an Elder in a church where I also served on the church board and in other roles (Mountain Christian Church in Joppa, Maryland). Mr. Johnson had the capacity of always being interested in other people, of always finding the positive in any issue (such as those being considered by the church board), of showing compassion toward others and their concerns, of always having a smile and seeming to always be where other people were brought together. He had a moderating influence on the discussions that took place in his presence and people listened when he spoke (which was neither continuous nor long). He always seemed to know when to speak and when to listen or ask questions of others.

There are others I think of in my life. My wife Jackie (we will celebrate our thirty-ninth anniversary this year) seems to know when to question me about actions I am contemplating. She knows when to encourage or to discourage an activity. She often introduces aspects of an issue that I had not yet considered. Or she helps me clarify an aspect that was on my mind but that I had not adequately thought through or was attempting to set aside. Because she is now a part of the team in our organization, she also has a broader influence on my daily work life as well as my personal life.

My parents, Adrian J. Oosting and Marguerite F. Oosting, are still an influence in my life. They live in North Muskegon, Michigan, where I grew up. In the last chapter, I mentioned that they are now ninety-six and ninety-four and have been married seventy-two years. My father remains interested in things around him by reading and talking with people on a wide range of topics. He and I share an interest in railroads, so we often talk about this when we are together. Both of my parents have a strong and abiding faith, but my mother is the one who will make a practical application by asking a question about a person's faith and obedience to God. She still plays the piano and I sing with her when we are together. Her faith is evident in the hymns she chooses to play and the way in which they are meaningful to her.

There are others. Dr. John L. McKinley was a professor at Muskegon Community College when I attended there. He, more than any other person, challenged me to think, to notice that there is a difference between fact and opinion or interpretation (he taught history and I then chose it as my undergraduate major). From him I learned more about when to question and when to know, how and where to seek knowledge and the value of books (and thus my love of libraries).

Most of us also have a public hero, a person we admire. Two persons who fit that category have probably never met each other, even though they are known to millions. One is Billy Graham, the evangelist, who has presented a public model of what a Christian can and should be in the midst of turmoil in this world and the challenges each of us faces every day.

Another is my sports hero, Al Kaline, who played for the Detroit Tigers during the fifties and sixties and was a member of the World Champion team in 1968. He is a model of a person who could think of his team rather than just himself, a person who represented a lifestyle that young players could model, and yet a person who excelled in the sport by winning the batting championship in the American League.

Who are your heroes? It could be interesting for you to reflect upon this and record as many as six of them on the lines below:

_____

_____

_____

_____

_____

_____

An underlying assumption about our choice of heroes that I chose not to mention until now is that the people we think of as role models or heroes are a direct reflection of our value systems (see Chapter Five). What we value in our lives is what we will value in the lives of others. What we might see in others is a living-out of what we are working on developing in our lives but feel we still have some distance to go before we are there. We like having a role model or hero because we know it can be done (they did it) and we have a benchmark by which we can assess how we are doing in our own personal development.

As a result, to determine our heroes or role models, we must draw upon our value systems. Our heroes then serve as guides for our personal development, so that we can come closer to being the persons our value systems tell us we would like to be.

Developing Relationships

Life is a series of relationships. Our first relationships are with our parents, our siblings, grandparents and other relatives of our generation and those of previous generations. We work our way through life until we are the older generation and our relationships are with our generation and younger ones. Outside of our families, we have relationships with those in school (and possibly college) and then with colleagues at work and friendships with others at church, in our neighborhood and in other ways that we relate to other human beings.

In all of these relationships there is a giving and a taking. As babies we are only taking while as mature Christians we might find ourselves mostly giving in our relationships. We depend upon some people. Some people depend upon us. Our children depend upon us early in their lives while late in our lives we might become dependent upon them. All of us need to receive from others for our fellowship, our mutual support, our worshiping together and the ability to give birth to children. We never get over the need to receive from others; but as mature Christians, that need to receive diminishes.

Our relationships offer us opportunities to serve others in many different ways over a long period of time. The way in which we serve is defined by the needs of the person or the needs of an organization (such as our churches) and is limited only by our abilities, talents, spiritual gifts, time and energy.

Human nature, as created by God, is such that we enjoy the company of other people. We tend to enjoy life more when we are around other people. As a result, we need to build relationships with our immediate families, other relatives, work associates and friends. Christians have a special group of friends they tend to see at least once a week while in Christian fellowship at a church. To strengthen these relationships we tend to do things for one another. We feel good about doing things for others and feel good when others do things for us. We don't all do the same things because our skills, talents, abilities and spiritual gifts differ.

Relationships are strongest when people enter a relationship interested in wanting to be of service to one another. This does not work if the attitude of one of the persons speaks of self-interest. When people perceive that others in a relationship are motivated primarily by self-interest, they too tend to withdraw and the relationship becomes remote at best. We can also see this in work situations. In some workplaces the workers are quite close to one another. In others the prevailing spirit is one of antagonism. In relationships the past is the best indicator of the present and future. Unless the situation is turned around through positive leadership, poor relationships only get worse.

As Christians we have a special responsibility to build relationships with others. Non-Christians are only introduced to the gospel through their contact with the Christian community. Thus, building bridges to non-Christians is very important in the evangelism effort. Christians also need to demonstrate the love that is central to Christianity. Christians have a special opportunity to demonstrate their love and compassion with fellow Christians. We sometimes fail at this as one group of Christians becomes so enamored with their theological stance or their form of worship that they begin to treat Christians with a different theology or form of worship as unworthy individuals. As long as all Christians use the New Testament as their guide in what the church should be, they should find common ground on most issues. Further, where the Bible speaks there must be unity. Where the Bible is silent, we can be different as long as the spirit of Christianity is honored.

Misunderstanding Each Other

Ken Voges and Ron Braund speak of how people misunderstand one another.[1] Oral and written communication is always imperfect. We sometimes do not say what we intend to say. In other situations we do not accurately hear what the other person said. Sometimes we hear the message accurately but do not fully understand it. Our choice of words, our body language, our timing, the physical setting, events of that hour and day — all will complicate the message. Some messages are simple ("Please hand me the salt") while others appear to be simple but are very complex ("I love you").

Then there is the matter of our wills. Sometimes we choose to avoid understanding what others say to us. This possibly happens most often when God is speaking to us. There are messages we don't want to hear. As a result, the message might be registered, but we pretend that we did not receive the message. Therefore, we take no action (or worse yet take a contrary action) like children sometimes do when we say, "Come here," and they run in the opposite direction. When we choose not to understand, we are the ones who pay most dearly for this miscommunication. But others pay as well. Sometimes it is an innocent party who is affected by our actions even though we did not anticipate this at the time we acted. Maturity requires that we do not avoid understanding messages just because we prefer to not receive them.

When we do not understand, it is not that we just lost the important message. It often means that we pick a different message in error that offends or upsets others. Thus the attempt at communication ends up pushing two persons or groups apart. Voges and Braund speak of the essentials in avoiding the misfortune of misunderstanding others. Their analysis is that each of us has a personality and lifestyle that affects how well we communicate.

It is likely that our ability to communicate effectively with others is closely related to our ability to communicate with ourselves. Are you open and honest with yourself? Do you rationalize many of your actions during a typical day so that you assume the acceptability of actions that are not consistent with your value system? Do you stop to think about yourself and your actions? Do you stop to think about your goals, about who you are and who you would like to be?

One of the themes of this book is that you will be a more rewarding person (to yourself and to others) if you take some time each day to think about yourself and in this process wrestle honestly with who you are and what you are doing. If you are unable or unwilling to do this, your ability to show compassion for others is very limited. It is a natural and psychologically healthy situation for each person to come to grips with the self (past, present and future). Psychologically healthy people can in turn help others, can show compassion that is real and that is understood and accepted by others. To show compassion you must come to understand the self first.

The Highest Level Of Maturity

The highest level of maturity for the Christian is to understand and accept the self (healthy self-concept), to be secure in one's salvation, to have one's basic needs for food, clothing and shelter met and to be focused upon helping others to meet their needs (showing compassion). Would that fit you? How many people do you know who could be described in this way? Possibly not many. Why do you think this might be so?

We have all probably met persons we consider to be mature Christians; however, even they have flaws. They are still human beings and thus have human imperfections.[2]

Are you moving toward Christian maturity? On what basis did you answer that question? How sure are you of your response?

There are many attributes that are common among mature Christians. We might say that a mature Christian is a person who:

- Is well read in the Bible, is familiar with and understands its contents.

- Prays every day, probably with a prayer journal that contains a list of people for whom he or she prays and the status of the request.

- Teaches other Christians in helping them to know the Lord.

- Earns the respect of other Christians as a man or woman of God.

- Is sought out by others to help them in times of need.

- Is capable of leadership in the church and willing to provide this leadership on both a continuing and as-needed basis.

- Is in fellowship and communion with other Christians through a local church.

- Is a relationship builder—not only with himself or herself but also between other pairs and groups of people.

- Is able to guide other Christians in a time of crisis in the church, personally, in the family or other places.

- Focuses always on Jesus rather than upon self and who tries to help others to have this focus without concern for his or her own image.

- Encourages others in their personal, family, career and other aspects of life.

- Is willing to give of the time which he or she has to help others.

- Is sure of his or her salvation and is interested in the opportunity to talk about it with others.

Douglass and Janssen speak of the need for the Christian to relate to other people, to show an interest in others, to understand others, to listen (be able to summarize what others have said) and to let other people know their perspectives have been considered.[3]

Areas For Compassion, Love, Leadership

Finding Opportunities

There might be times when you feel that you would really like to help other people but you don't know where to start. Or you might question whether you have the abilities or spiritual gifts (see Chapter Four) to help others. This could be a rationalization on your part to justify why you are not doing those things. Here are some things you can do in your community or area to help others:

- Contact your minister and talk with him or her about the needs of people in the church and about needs in the community in general.

- Look in the telephone pages under churches, church supplies and services, and religious organizations.

- If you have ever been involved in a charity before, make contact with them again.

- Talk with another Christian you respect as an individual well connected in the community. Ask him or her where the needs are.

- There is probably a homeless shelter, a place for battered women, a center for troubled youth in your community if your city has 100,000 or more in population. If your community is smaller, check anyway with the city government. If you can't find a phone number there that is helpful, call the mayor's office.

- Look at your neighborhood. Do you know these people? If not, get acquainted. In doing so you are likely to find a need. It might not result in a major project, but possibly something like a retired person who lives alone and would enjoy a fresh-baked loaf of bread from time to time or a phone call to see if they are OK.

Are you active in your own church? If you have an interest in missions work, for example, you might go to the next meeting of the missions committee. If the time isn't announced in the bulletin, ask the church secretary or the minister. If not missions, pick another committee and get involved.

Do many people know who you are? If not, get better acquainted with people wherever you go. And do go, go places, meet people, do things.

Providing Service

Compassion, love, leadership. All are forms of service. Service is an attitude. Are you more comfortable in serving others or in being served? Are you willing to exert the effort required to help others? Providing service is being a servant. Are you comfortable in being a servant? If you are feeling that you are not sure, read a book on the life of Christ. He was the master servant. He washed feet,[4] taught[5] and healed.[6] Why did He do these things? What motivated Christ to do these things? What motivates you today? Would you like to be a Christian servant?

Providing service to others begins with a recognition of where your talents, abilities, spiritual gifts and skills rest (see Chapter Four). If you are a skilled electrician, on your day off you might help others who are unable to pay and might have unsafe electrical conditions in their homes that need correcting. Maybe your role should be in teaching or leadership in your local church. Most churches are in need of leadership. Look at the list provided above to determine where you might serve. Perhaps you are already serving in some capacity. Is there some opportunity to expand service in this area? The key is to find the area of service that makes sense for you (something you can do well, enjoy doing and can do without undue personal sacrifice) and then make a commitment to God and to yourself as to exactly what you are willing to do as a servant of the Lord.

A Means Of Extending Self

God has blessed you. Look around you to discover the ways. Think about the experiences you have had. How might you extend yourself to help bless others?

As Christians we need to reach out to others even though we will not always be appreciated and often not recognized.[7] Our service to others is not motivated by the recognition we will receive on this earth. We are serving God through other people. If we are primarily motivated by the praise we receive from others, we have not yet arrived at the point when our focus is on others rather than the self. We all like to receive praise and it does give us confirmation that we are on the right path. But our goals, if we are to genuinely show compassion for others, are focused on what we can do to make the lives of other persons more spiritually, physically or psychologically rewarding for them.

Extending yourself to others requires courage. In Chapter Nine we talked about courage. Just as we all have different personalities, we all have different levels of courage. In fact, the two are related. However, some people, who by nature tend to be shy, are sometimes people of great courage. How can this be? This is often because their faith, their compassion, their commitment is so strong that their courage exceeds what their personalities would suggest that their courage level might be. Be a person of great faith, great compassion and great commitment and you will be looking for places to affect the lives of others. You will have given yourself great courage.

The Rewards

Our greatest reward is in heaven. The Scriptures tell us that, in return for our belief, we have eternal salvation.[8] There is no greater reward that any human being can receive. In addition to our belief, we are encouraged to live as Jesus would.[9] What does it mean to use Jesus as our example and guide? It means that we strive to come close to the blameless life that Jesus led on earth. This means to show love, kindness, helpfulness, leadership, courage, compassion, doing our share and more. As we demonstrate compassion toward others, we are being more Christlike. Being able to be genuinely compassionate toward others is a sign of the mature Christian.

The random act of kindness returns — the recently received graduation announcement or the knowledge that you helped a person even if they do not give it recognition. Thomas Jefferson gave us the phrase, "pursuit of happiness." We would all like to be happy, I am convinced, even though some of us are confirmed grouches. Happiness is the stage in life when we feel secure. We are pleased with who we are, with the people around us (physically and psychologically) and our relationship with the Lord. When we achieve this state, it is natural for us to reach out to others. In so doing, we show compassion and thus help others to achieve this same happiness. When we do this without expecting or hoping for personal gain in return, we are truly extending ourselves to others; we are showing compassion just as Jesus Christ demonstrated compassion for us.

Some persons do not thank others because their own self-concepts need repair. They are hurting because they have not developed an appreciation for their own abilities or the opportunities they have to live in positive, dynamic relationships with others.

A more vibrant you is a person you will enjoy more and others will enjoy being around. This includes being positive, joyful and praising God for the opportunities He has provided.

Endnotes

[1]Ken Voges and Ron Braund, *Understanding How Others Misunderstand You: A Unique And Proven Plan For Strengthening Personal Relationships*, Foreword by Charles Stanley (Chicago, IL: Moody Press, 1990), pp. 11-30.

[2] "Who is wise and understanding among you? Let him show it by his good life, by deeds done in the humility that comes from wisdom. But if you harbor bitter envy and selfish ambition in your hearts, do not boast about it or deny the truth. Such 'wisdom' does not come down from heaven but is earthly,

unspiritual, of the devil. For where you have envy and selfish ambition, there you find disorder and every evil practice" (James 3:13-16). See also James 4:1-3: "What causes fights and quarrels among you? Don't they come from your desires that battle within you? You want something but don't get it. You kill and covet, but you cannot have what you want. You quarrel and fight. You do not have, because you do not ask God. When you ask, you do not receive, because you ask with wrong motives, that you may spend what you get on your pleasures."

[3] Steve Douglass and Al Janssen, *How To Achieve Your Potential And Enjoy Life!* (San Bernardino, CA: Here's Life Publishers, 1987), pp. 41-49.

[4] "After that, he poured water into a basin and began to wash his disciples' feet, drying them with the towel that was wrapped around him" (John 13:5).

[5] "Jesus returned to Galilee in the power of the Spirit, and news about him spread through the whole countryside. He taught in their synagogues, and everyone praised him" (Luke 4:15).

[6] The first healings are recorded in Matthew 8, Mark 3, Luke 4 and John 4. The four Gospels contain numerous references to this aspect of Jesus' ministry.

[7] "Let us not become weary in doing good, for at the proper time we will reap a harvest if we do not give up. Therefore, as we have opportunity, let us do good to all people, especially to those who belong to the family of believers" (Galatians 6:9-10).

[8] "For God did not appoint us to suffer wrath but to receive salvation through our Lord Jesus Christ" (1 Thessalonians 5:9).

[9] "To this you were called, because Christ suffered for you, leaving you an example, that you should follow in his steps" (1 Peter 2:21).

Chapter Eleven

Self-Discipline And Attitudes

Life is not meant to be endured, but to be enjoyed. — David Jeremiah

Self-discipline is the means by which we control our thoughts and actions so as to direct our resources toward the accomplishment of our goals. — Kenneth W. Oosting

Character is not what we have done, but who we are. — Bill Hybels

In the years spent researching "I Love Life," I have interviewed hundreds of Good Samaritans. They are in every city and town in this nation, but many go unnoticed as they perform their good deeds. Most of them do not seek publicity and wish to remain anonymous. Mary Catherine Strobel was one of them. She never sought interviews or recognition during her years of volunteer service in Nashville. The people who were most aware of her were those she was trying to help. — Jerry Dahmen

What Does Self-Discipline Mean?

Discipline

When we first think of the word discipline, we think of it as something that we apply to children to force them to comply with what we consider to be acceptable behavior. Let's look at that concept for a few moments.

First, there is "acceptable behavior." This is our "goal." We want children to behave in a way that meets our "goals." Among other things this probably includes practicing good manners, not being too loud, avoiding anything unsafe, putting toys away after playtime is over, eating their meals, responding to adult requests and gradually assuming more responsibility for their own actions.

Second, there is the element of "force" by which we ensure that children will do what we want them to do. If they do not, we introduce another concept—that of penalty. The penalty, whether it be a spanking or denial of a privilege, is applied when a child fails to comply with the expected behavior. The purpose of the penalty is to reinforce with the child that next time he or she had better do what the discipliner expects. The result, we hope, is that the child sees that compliance is the better choice both now and in the future.

Third, there is the element of "we apply to" which means that one person (the parent, grandparent or teacher) is applying the discipline to another person (the child). In this situation the person doing the applying sets the goals while the other person accepts them. As children get older, we let them participate more fully in setting these goals.

There is another kind of discipline of others which we sometimes call "peer pressure." In this situation, one person puts pressure upon another person to conform to certain behaviors. You might have heard, "You're not going to wear that to church, are you?" The typical response is to reexamine what you planned to wear and likely change into something else. We are all affected by people in general, but especially by specific persons close to us. A few people enjoy being eccentric by exercising behavior outside the accepted norms. But most of us are content to act within these boundaries. An interesting book (and workbook) on this topic is *Boundaries, When to Say Yes, When to Say No, To Take Control of Your Life* by Dr. Henry Cloud and Dr. John Townsend.[1]

When we respond to the pressures of society and those persons around us, we are moving from disciplining others to self-discipline because we are now making the choices of when to conform and when to be at least partly nonconforming.

Self-Discipline

Now, what happens if we add "self" in front of the word "discipline"? This changes the person to whom the discipline is applied and the person who will enforce it. Both become us. We gauge the behavior of ourselves and we are the ones to apply any penalties for failure to comply with acceptable behavior. We become our own policemen. What is the obvious problem with such a system?

If we choose against "acceptable behavior" which helps us toward our "goals" in the first place, where will the incentive come from to apply any "penalty" for this lack of "compliance?" Pressure that we might feel from God's Word is our first source. Our consciences are also a source. Another is in the form of commitments we make to others ("I'll be there at four" or "I'll see that this is taken care of properly"). Let's look at each of these three **both** in terms of setting our goals (standards, behaviors) and the self-discipline we exercise in meeting these goals.

The Role of God's Word

Our belief in God is based upon a "respect" or "fear" of Him and His Word. Therefore, Christians take the Holy Bible as the most important guide for who and what they should be as well as what they should do and say. This is as it should be. While Christians take this as a given, we are limited by several factors:

- Most of us have a limited knowledge of the Bible.
- Most of us lack understanding of many aspects of the Scripture.
- Most of us do little each day to correct #1 and #2.
- Most of us lack the self-discipline to become better Christians by a program of regular Bible reading and seeking to increase our understanding of the Scripture.

Fortunately, if we attend church on Sunday morning and Sunday School and maybe a midweek service, we are getting some of the knowledge and understanding that we need to have a meaningful Christian faith. But even that assumes that we are attentive to what we hear and that we participate directly in activities such as a Bible study with the goal of learning. Attending a church service once a week and falling asleep during the sermon will do little to vitalize our Christian faith.

Volumes have been written on what the Holy Bible directs us to do in our daily lives. Volumes have also been written on what the Holy Bible tells us about self-discipline, about what we should do to ensure that we live godly lives. We will not attempt here to list what the Scripture tells us except to say:

- Scripture is the guide for our behavior.

- Scripture is the guide for our self-discipline to enforce that we actually behave as we should.

You are serious about wanting to live a life that is God-directed or you wouldn't be taking the time to read this book. Assuming this, what then do you do next? May I suggest the following:

- Enter into a program of systematic Bible study. Most of us can do this best by being a part of a group which studies the Bible on a regular basis. This should be supplemented by a program of daily Bible reading which you do on a regular basis—a process that, by the way, requires considerable self-discipline.

- Enter into a time of daily devotions and prayer. This need not be long, but it needs to be regular. A prayer journal in which you record your prayer concerns for that day will be helpful. Reference to your daily Bible reading will likely be helpful.

- Find a prayer partner. It is essential that this be a person who shares your concern for prayer and who shares your self-discipline to set aside some time on a periodic basis to pray with you. I attend a breakfast meeting every Friday morning of the Fellowship of Companies for Christ (except when I am traveling or speaking elsewhere). During this hour we have about thirty minutes to voice prayer concerns and then we lift those matters up in prayer. The other half hour is devoted to the study of a topic (related to a book or the Scripture) that is helpful to these Christian men and women who own or manage their own businesses.

The Scripture can lead us both in what our thoughts and behaviors should be as well as in how we might discipline ourselves to conform to the teachings we find there.

Our Consciences

Our consciences can be a powerful tool on our behalf. Our consciences are a reflection of our value systems.[2] Our consciences will then reflect our Christian faith. The most important single factor in our consciences will be our Christian faith. To that we add our own sense of what is right and wrong, the desires, impact and requests of others and our own sense of who we are.

We vary, however, in how much we are willing to let our consciences guide us. It is natural for us to put up barriers to protect what we think needs protecting. Sometimes we set up psychological barriers that prevent even us from seeing deeply into our own personal makeups. J. Grant Howard has written an excellent book[3] to help us to understand what we do. Dr.

Howard explains that we set up shields or barriers to avoid the trauma of letting others and ourselves see the real us. This trauma of transparency refers to the difficulty we experience when we become more transparent and allow others to see the real persons inside ourselves. We set up these barriers for ourselves. We say "I don't want to think about that" to escape the possibility of addressing issues within us. As we move toward feeling comfortable with transparency, we are moving toward Christian maturity.

Our consciences have a very neat feature. When we begin to behave in ways that run counter to our value systems, our consciences act up. We fight our consciences with rationalizations. Have you ever used the rationalization "Everybody does it" or "It's no big deal" when you are putting money back into your wallet or purse in the parking lot outside a store and your conscience registers that the clerk gave you too much change and that you need to walk back into the store to return the extra money? Rationalization tells you it is not worth the effort to follow your conscience.

Several years ago my wife Jackie and I were driving along in Panama City, Florida, when all of a sudden it hit me that I had not paid for the item I had just selected in a store about five miles back. We turned around and went back and paid the amount that was due. It had been an error, and fortunately the sequence of events finally processed in my mind so that I could correct the situation. But it would have been easy to keep on going by rationalizing that "things like that will happen" or "it was under $5.00." Our consciences tell us that the amount has nothing to do with the issue. What has to do with it is that we did not do right and that we need to correct it.

There is a fine line between a rationalization and a lie. Both will come back to haunt us and neither establishes a neat system that we can explain to others on a consistent basis. When we rationalize, we argue with ourselves by saying that something that is wrong is really all right because of (whatever we can think of at the time). In a lie, we argue with ourselves by saying that whatever we are saying is all right (even though we know it is not true) because the situation is unfair, because we really want something or maybe because we don't care).

Christians can never, ever lie. Christians can never make statements that are designed to lead others to a wrong conclusion by leaving out facts or embellishing the truth. We can never purposely deceive others. If we do, we face some specific problems.

- First, we are behaving in a manner that is inconsistent with our faith. We cannot witness to others when we are ourselves in deceit.

- Second, we are in conflict with our value systems. The values of a Christian must include following the teachings of Jesus Christ. This leaves no room for dishonesty in any form (a lie is a form of dishonesty). When we behave in conflict with our value systems, we must deal with our consciences. Our consciences will set off bells and other signals to tell us that all is not right.

- Third, deceit and having goals do not mesh well. When we state a goal that we know is dependent upon deceit, we are facing our own duplicity, our own cheating. Deceit works more easily with spur of the moment rationalization. Thus, if we are to rely upon deceit, we are likely to be without goals. Having goals is a major theme of this book. If you are determined to live by deceit, this book cannot help you much; you need to turn to Proverbs or another part of the Scripture that will guide you in turning from this type of behavior.

- Fourth, when the Judgment Day comes, what will you tell God?

- Fifth, when you tell a lie, it is difficult to remember what story you told to what person. If you tell the truth, it is the same for every person.

The easiest lie to tell is one we tell to ourselves. There is no other person to challenge us unless our behavior based upon the lie is evident to others. When we lie to ourselves, we most often do this in the form of rationalization by arguing "Who will know?" or "Who cares?" Deception of the self is probably even more destructive than deceiving others. This tears at our very core, our value systems, our ability to relate to others. It makes having personal or professional goals nearly impossible. We can always lie to ourselves that we have already reached a goal, so why exert any more effort? If this is a problem in your life, pray about it.

Closely related to this and to our next topic (commitments to others) is the issue of what then do we tell to others. We do not have to be an open book to others in the sense that we tell everyone everything we know. Why is this?

- In the first place, they don't want to know everything you know; don't bore people with your attempt at being honest.

- Second, don't be a gossip. A gossip takes pleasure in being the first to tell something that others do not know regardless of the impact of what is said.

- Third, be sensitive. If one person makes a negative remark about another person, it is not your duty to repeat this to the person who is being spoken about.

- Fourth, be discreet. If information is shared with you in confidence, it is not your duty in life to share this with others. If someone asks you not to share information, be careful about what you promise. For example, if you become aware of an illegal activity, you must ethically report it to avoid being an accomplice to the activity. Or, if you are in business, you are not obligated to tell your competition what you plan to do.

- Fifth, be sure you have all the pertinent facts before you speak. One small piece of information known to you might be very much out of context and lead to unfair conclusions.

Commitments We Make To Others

All of us make commitments to others. As Christians, we should make only those commitments that we have a reasonable capability and intent of keeping. We must exercise self-discipline, then, in what we promise, in the commitments we make to others.

Each of us will be challenged to do more than we can physically and psychologically accomplish. We must make some choices. We must, in that process, be persons of integrity. Integrity means that when we say we will do something, we will make every reasonable effort to do it (being kept from it only by factors beyond our control, such as illness or a true emergency in which another person requires our immediate help).

The issue of integrity requires some additional attention at this point. A person of integrity is respected by others and by himself or herself. This is sometimes referred to as character or the moral fiber of which we are made. A Christian must be a person of integrity, of sound character, or he or she will have a number of problems:

- First, we will not be at peace with God. Refer to the book by Rev. Billy Graham on this topic.[4] Every Christian must seek a harmony with God that results from righteous living based upon a deep and abiding Christian faith. If you lack this peace with God, exert all the energy you have to find it. Seek the counsel of others, read the Scripture and pray.

- Second, in order to set goals, your own personal life cannot be in disarray. Being a person of integrity is essential to having your life in order. It is difficult for order to come from chaos. Not being a person of integrity means that your life is in chaos. Find order in your life and you will be able to establish both personal and professional goals.

- Third, you will be able to affect the lives of others positively. You can witness to them about your faith, you can guide them to set goals for themselves, you can help them through difficult times in their lives and you can be a solid example that others will use in the development of their lives. Each of us is watched by countless others and they are guided in part by what they see. What kind of influence are you having on the lives of others right now?

- Fourth, you have the potential of being at peace with yourself. This is a great feeling. Probably none of us can stay at peace with ourselves as we face struggles in life, but these are precious times in which we feel contentment knowing that we are striving to be the persons God would want us to be and that we are reasonably satisfied that we are on the right track in this quest.

The Effect Of Attitude

Each of us has a personality. This personality is a pattern of behavior in how we relate to the experiences of life. We initiate or cause some of these experiences to happen. Others are the result of the actions of others or of natural causes (or a combination). Attitude is one aspect of personality, the way in which we see the world around us.

Each of us has had the experience of witnessing a person who becomes very angry at the slightest provocation and another who calmly listens without anger in a situation when another person is being very unfair in their treatment of others. These two situations could even be the same person under different circumstances at different times. Why does our attitude toward life vary from time to time?

Some of us are usually pictures of sunshine and some of us are natural grouches. Someone bought a sign a few years ago for my parents' home which read, "Here lives a very nice lady and an old grouch." Because my father also has a good sense of humor, he knew who the grouch was. Most of us are fairly consistent in our attitude although there might be two sides (like before and after the first morning coffee). Christians should have a view of life that will look for the good, the ideal, in every situation. Some Christians experience depression and might wish to consult *Happiness is a Choice, The Symptoms, Causes and Cures of Depression* by Frank Minirith and Paul Meier.[5]

You might study the Gospels for glimpses into the attitude of Jesus. Jesus was angry when he overturned the tables in the temple, but most of the time he was very positive. His attitude was always appropriate for the situation. How often can we say that about ourselves?

Attitude determines our approach to life. Eugenia Price has described what we can learn from each of the Gospels about learning to live.[6] Jerry Dahmen in *I Love Life, In Spite Of It All*[7] describes people who have faced great difficulties and still found a way to have a positive attitude. The quote from *I Love Life* at the beginning of this chapter is about Mary Catherine Strobel who was a notable person in her self-discipline and her positive, Christian attitude toward helping others. She became a role model for the rest of us.[8]

Our attitudes are a reflection of our self-esteem, which also deeply affects our overall personality. The Christian has reason to be self-confident. Christ died on the cross for our sins. We are forgiven. God is always with us. He created us in His image. God has a plan for our lives. He has created a beautiful earth on which we can live out our existence. There are great Christians with whom we can associate. For further reading on this subject, I would like to suggest *The Dilemma Of Self-Esteem, The Cross and Christian Confidence* by Joanna and Alister McGrath.[9]

The foes in our attitudes toward effective self-discipline include rationalization, indulgence, laziness, self-centeredness and apathy. All these attributes stem from a value system that says whatever is good for me in the short run is what I want. This is a value system that is inconsistent with a viable Christian faith. We cannot read the New Testament without understanding that we are to place our faith in God (not ourselves) and we are to serve others (ourselves after God and others). All of us face attitudinal issues and thus value system problems in being effectively self-disciplined. This means we have a constant struggle as we seek to place God first in our lives and to be of service to others.

There is some cost involved in disciplining ourselves. There might be something that we personally would really like to have or would like to do or become. We come to realize, however, that relenting to that satisfaction would mean sacrificing something that is even more important to us. Self-discipline means satisfying the aspects of our life that have the highest value and priority regardless of immediate needs and desires and to do so consistently over a long period of time.

When we are self-disciplined, there is also some benefit. We are more likely to be relaxed (having resolved some internal conflicts) which in turn allows us to focus even more on the ultimate prize. Second, we are more likely to be satisfied with ourselves and thus have a higher sense of self-esteem. We are likely to put ourselves down if we say we will do something important and then do not get around to doing it. We failed because we lacked self-discipline. More on this in the next section. Third, the perception of others will be enhanced as they see that we have the ability to discipline ourselves to do as we intend, as we say we will do. Other people will admire self-discipline even when they do not relate to the values that we are maintaining. For example, we might admire a person who consistently sets aside twenty minutes for exercise each morning even when we personally might not feel that this amount of time for exercise is important. We admire the person's self-discipline to set aside the twenty minutes and then stick to it.

Personal Values Relate To Personal Control

Bill Hybels refers to self-discipline as "achieving success through delaying gratification."[10] Gratification relates to satisfying personal desires. Not all personal desires can be met, but without self-discipline we spent much of our time, energy and resources trying to meet as many personal desires as possible.

It is important to point out here that there is a significant difference between needs and desires. When we rationalize, we confuse the two by thinking that all things we want are needs. We **need** what is essential for a satisfactory lifestyle. We **want** what is better.

Self-Discipline And Goals/Priorities

Self-discipline allows us to set goals with a reasonable expectation that the goals will be met. A person with self-discipline can set long-term and complex goals and expect to achieve most of them. The person with self-discipline in his or her value system will be able to focus the available energy, time and other resources on the things that matter most. As a result, that person will achieve more of his or her long-term goals.

A person with self-discipline but without goals is like a beautiful new car that sits in the garage with no place to go. We have the vehicle but lack direction. The two must go together in order for either of them to be meaningful in our lives.

Self-Discipline And Accomplishment

Accomplishment is the fulfillment of a goal. Very few meaningful things are accomplished accidentally. Accomplishment is the result of a reasonable goal that is pursued through self-discipline that allows your energies, time and other resources to be applied directly and consistently to the goal. The result is the accomplishment of the goal.

Self-Discipline And Faith

The Relationship Between Self-Discipline and Faith

Applying self-discipline to our Christian faith is substantively different than applying self-discipline to our personal and professional goals. Here the goals are supplied for us. Proverbs and the writings of Paul are particularly rich resources for direction in our Christian faith. It is then up to us to apply the self-discipline to see that these things happen in our lives. Thus, once we believe, the fruits of our faith are closely tied to the self-discipline that we apply to that faith.

Advice From Proverbs

The Book of Proverbs was written as words of wisdom to be shared so that our lives might be lived wisely in the sight of God. A few examples from Proverbs include:

- Listen, my son, to your father's instruction and do not forsake your mother's teaching. They will be a garland to grace your head and a chain to adorn your neck. — Proverbs 1:8-9
- My son, if you accept my words and store up my commands within you, turning your ear to wisdom and applying your heart to understanding, and if you call out for insight and cry aloud for understanding, and if you look for it as for silver and search for it as for hidden treasure, then you will understand the fear of the Lord and find the knowledge of God. — Proverbs 2:1-5
- My son, preserve sound judgment and discernment, do not let them out of your sight. — Proverbs 3:21

- Do not forsake wisdom, and she will protect you; love her, and she will watch over you. — Proverbs 4:6
- Go to the ant, you sluggard; consider its ways and be wise! It has no commander, no overseer or ruler, yet it stores its provisions in summer and gathers its food at harvest. — Proverbs 6:6-8
- For these commands are a lamp, this teaching is a light, and the corrections of discipline are the way to life. — Proverbs 6:23
- Instruct a wise man and he will be wiser still; teach a righteous man and he will add to his learning. — Proverbs 9:9
- Lazy hands make a man poor, but diligent hands bring wealth. — Proverbs 10:4
- He who heeds discipline shows the way to life, but whoever ignores correction leads others astray. — Proverbs 10:17
- When pride comes, then comes disgrace, but with humility comes wisdom. — Proverbs 11:2
- The truly righteous man attains life, but he who pursues evil goes to his death. — Proverbs 11:19
- A wife of noble character is her husband's crown, but a disgraceful wife is like decay in his bones. — Proverbs 12:4
- Dishonest money dwindles away, but he who gathers money little by little makes it grow. — Proverbs 13:11
- A wise man fears the Lord and shuns evil, but a fool is hotheaded and reckless. — Proverbs 14:16
- A gentle answer turns away wrath, but a harsh word stirs up anger. — Proverbs 15:1
- Plans fail for lack of counsel, but with many advisers they succeed. — Proverbs 15:22
- If a man pays back evil for good, evil will never leave his house. — Proverbs 17:13
- A fool finds no pleasure in understanding but delights in airing his own opinions. — Proverbs 18:2
- One who is slack in his work is brother to one who destroys." — Proverbs 18:9

- He who gets wisdom loves his own soul; he who cherishes understanding prospers. — Proverbs 19:8
- Do not love sleep or you will grow poor; stay awake and you will have food to spare. — Proverbs 20:13
- He who pursues righteousness and love finds life, prosperity and honor. — Proverbs 21:21
- A good name is more desirable than great riches; to be esteemed is better than silver or gold. — Proverbs 22:1
- Do not envy wicked men, do not desire their company. — Proverbs 24:1
- A word aptly spoken is like apples of gold in settings of silver. — Proverbs 25:11
- Do not boast about tomorrow, for you do not know what a day may bring forth. — Proverbs 27:1
- He who tends a fig tree WILL eat its fruit, and he who looks after his master will be honored. — Proverbs 27:18
- When a country is rebellious, it has many rulers, but a man of understanding and knowledge maintains order…Evil men do not understand justice, but those who seek the Lord understand it fully. — Proverbs 28:2, 5
- Keep falsehood and lies far from me; give me neither poverty nor riches, but give me only my daily bread. Otherwise, I may have too much and disown you and say, "Who is the Lord?" Or I may become poor and steal, and so dishonor the name of my God. — Proverbs 30:8, 9

Advice From The New Testament

There are passages in the New Testament as well that direct our attention toward self-discipline in our behavior. One of these is in Romans 12:1-2 which reads: "Therefore, I urge you, brothers, in view of God's mercy, to offer your bodies as living sacrifices, holy and pleasing to God — this is your spiritual act of worship. Do not conform any longer to the pattern of this world, but be transformed by the renewing of your mind. Then you will be able to test and approve what God's will is — his good, pleasing and perfect will." Here we are encouraged toward the self-discipline of our bodies, our physical being. Further, we are urged against conforming to this world. Instead we are to discipline ourselves to follow God through the renewing of our minds. A powerful thought. There are many other admonitions in this chapter to bolster our self-discipline.

Romans 13 talks about submission to authorities. It is tempting for us to answer only to ourselves, but we must discipline ourselves to answer to others as well.

First Corinthians 6:1-8 directs us to discipline ourselves to avoid lawsuits with another believer and to "flee from sexual immorality."[11] Read 1 Corinthians 6:12 for maybe the strongest statement in the New Testament about self-discipline.[12] Here Paul is likely referring to a person in the church at Corinth who had said that he had permission to do anything. Paul responds with a lesson in self-discipline when he says, "but not everything is beneficial." Paul goes on in this chapter to talk about "the body" is "for the Lord."[13] He admonishes the church to have the self-discipline to follow this teaching.

My Plan For Self-Discipline

What is your plan for self-discipline? The major theme of this book is action—by you. The book presents the need for each of us to have both personal and professional goals, priorities among those goals and strategies for making them happen. But the best plans, in themselves, do not produce results. This is where self-discipline, the theme of this chapter, enters the picture. Self-discipline is essential to the realization of your goals and strategies.

The expectation of this chapter is that by this point you are sufficiently motivated to evaluate your own resolve for self-discipline. Self-discipline is not a goal that is done once for all time. It becomes a way of life; it affects everything that we do and how we accomplish every goal.

Self-discipline asks the question, "Who is in control of my life?" If no one is, then expect terrible results. When others are in control of our lives, then we can expect that what we do will be determined by others. If we are in control of our own lives, then we need to have direction, focus, goals. Only self-discipline to focus our efforts on those directions, that focus or those goals will allow us to realize God's will and our desires for our lives.

Endnotes

[1]Grand Rapids, MI: Zondervan, 1992.

[2]See Chapter 5.

[3]J. Grant Howard, *The Trauma of Transparency, A Biblical Approach to Interpersonal Communication* (Franklin, TN: JKO Publishing, 1997—see inside the front cover for JKO Publishing ordering information).

[4]Billy Graham, *Peace With God* (Dallas, TX: Word Publishing, 1988).

[5]Grand Rapids, MI: Baker Books, 1994.

[6]Eugenia Price, *Learning to Live*, Reprint Edition (New York, NY: Jove Publications, 1986).

[7]Nashville, TN: Broadman-Holman, 1989.

[8]Ibid., 77-83.

[9]Wheaton, IL: Crossway Books, 1992.

[10]Bill Hybels, *Who You Are When No One's Looking: Choosing Consistency, Resisting Compromise* (Downers Grove, IL: InterVarsity Press, 1987), 23-33. Hybels devotes one chapter to the subject of discipline.

[11]1 Corinthians 6:18.

[12]"'Everything is permissible for me'—but not everything is beneficial. 'Everything is permissible for me'—but I will not be mastered by anything."

[13]1 Corinthians 6:13.

Chapter Twelve

Effective Personal Management

The rigorous pursuit of our day is the search for dignity and personal worth. It is a mighty quest fueled by the flames of passion that burn in the souls of people who refuse to surrender to the voices which declare we are nothing. — R. C. Sproul[1]

(People) have very gradually become disturbed over permissiveness, pornography, the public schools, the breakdown of the family and finally abortion. But they have not seen this as a totality — each thing being a part, a symptom, of a much larger problem. They have failed to see that all of this has come about due to a shift in world view — that is, through a fundamental change in the overall way people think and view the world and life as a whole. This shift has been **away from** *a world view that was at least vaguely Christian in people's memory (even if they were not individually Christian)* **toward** *something completely different — toward a world view based upon the idea that the final reality is impersonal matter or energy shaped into its present*

form by impersonal chance. – Francis A. Schaeffer[2] (emphasis that of the author)

Since Jesus Christ, the Son of God, took upon himself the role of servant, so must we. – Charles R. Swindoll[3]

Wisdom is supreme; therefore get wisdom. Though it cost all you have, get understanding. – Proverbs 4:7

Each of us does search for "dignity and personal worth" (see quote from R. C. Sproul above). We differ in how hot those "flames of passion" are in our search. In this book I have attempted to encourage you to increase your passion and to provide you with a framework for putting that passion in you to work on your behalf (and thus affecting everyone who has any contact with you).

The world in which we do our searching is described in the quote above from Francis A. Schaeffer. This world view is presently changing from a vaguely Christian one to one in which everyone defines what is right without a deep concern for the anarchy that results in a society that places an extreme emphasis upon individual rights . In Christ we put God as the head – as the guide, as the focus – instead of ourselves. If Christians differ from other people in any way, it must be that our faith in God puts God first and everything else second, including the self. This has tremendous implications for how we should live, as Schaeffer points out in his writings.

The quote from Charles R. Swindoll above takes this a step further. Our concern for ourselves does not even merit second place. If we are to be servants, we must improve our serve as Swindoll suggests.

In all we do we must seek wisdom and understanding. It is only from this platform that we are able to serve God, serve others and direct our own lives as God would have us be directed. The platform must be solid and be based upon faith and other personal values that in fact guide our daily behavior. Seeking wisdom and understanding are essential to a solid platform.

Review Of The Prerequisites

The purpose of this book was outlined in Chapter One with the presentation of twelve prerequisites for managing yourself. The concept of prerequisites is that there are areas that must be mastered before you can effectively manage yourself, before you can be in control of your own life. Those prerequisites are:

- Being right with God
- Being right with the world; being a servant; relationships are OK
- Being in control of self
- Discovering and acting on personal values consistent with your Christian faith
- Discovering self and being that person
- Knowing and using your spiritual gifts
- Setting goals and following them
- Setting priorities within your goals and acting on your priorities
- Learning continuously
- Being of great courage—taking considered and consistent risks
- Acting consistently with your faith and other values over a long period of time
- Assuming responsibility—being in charge of your present and future

Addressing these prerequisites for managing yourself has been the focus of the previous chapters. In an early draft of these prerequisites, I presented them as areas in which we must be willing to take action. By the time I completed this last chapter, two years later, I describe them as actions we are in fact taking in our lives. There is an important distinction.

Willingness to take charge of your life is far different from having done it. To say you are willing to act is different from saying you have done something. When you have acted, you have proven your willingness. When you state a willingness, there is still some doubt about the clarity of your goals, the setting of your priorities and the self-discipline that is necessary to follow through to make them happen.

If you have read the earlier chapters, you have a pretty good idea now of whether or not you meet the prerequisites stated above. You know if you are willing to be honest with yourself where you fall short, where you have work to do. In this chapter my goal is to help you address those issues with goals, priorities and actions consistent with your value system.

Christian Faith And Its Impact

Prerequisite number one is "Being right with God." By that we mean that not only is our faith intact but our relationships with God have given us a deep sense of peace with God. We are not blaming God, criticizing God, arguing with God or mad at God. In human relationships both persons in the relationship can change to affect the relationship. In the relationship with God, God does not change. That means that when the relationship sours, we must look at ourselves. When it improves it is because we took the initiative to have the relationship improve. God offers Himself to us; it is up to us to determine what we will make of our relationships with Him.

Each of us is created with a self-will. In that self-will we are capable of many thoughts and emotions. We can act in many different ways. God did not create us this way by accident. This means that if we are close to God, we have made a deliberate choice for that to occur. God does not make this decision, but He is always there. We must decide that our faith will be strong and that it will have an impact upon our lives.

Just think. We can have a relationship with God, and we get to determine how close it will be. What decision in our lives could be more important?

If there are barriers in your life which prevent you from having a close relationship with God, what are they? Anger, bitterness, apathy, busyness, self-centeredness? If it is anger, what are you going to do about it? If it is self-centeredness, what are you going to do about it? What does the Bible direct you to do?

God has a will for each of us. It is our responsibility to discover it and act upon it. How is your discovery going?

Earlier chapters provide you with some suggestions about where to start in discovering God's will and building the right relationships with God and others. But whether you follow the suggestions in this book or not, take the appropriate action. Do it today, right now.

Discovering And Dealing With The World

The second prerequisite says: Being right with the world; being a servant; relationships are OK.

It is one thing to be right with God; it is another to be right with everyone in the world. God did not create just one of us, He created millions of us. He put us all on the same planet. He must have intended that we would get along.

It is easy for us to say that world peace is for others to determine. Yet threats to world peace in Gaza or in China or in South Africa or in our own city are often begun by one person or just a few people. What can we do? There are many opportunities to contribute to the work of people or organizations who are acting to deal with these problems. Just a few examples of groups that help people are: World Vision, Feed the Children, the American Red Cross, missions organizations like Christian Missionary Fellowship, SIM and the United States Center for World Mission as well as your own local church with its outreach programs. Decide how you will help.

Closer to home and facing us directly every day are our relationships with others around us. This is where we address whether we are right with the world, whether we have the hearts of servants, whether our relationships with others are at least OK. How do we know whether we are OK in this department? Answer the following questions:

- Am I currently angry with one or more persons?
- Do I have any enemies? Are there people with whom I do not speak? Are there people I avoid?
- Do I have a positive outlook on the world?

- What is the ratio between my complaining and my praising when it relates to other people?
- What was the last significant thing I did that was intended for the benefit of others?
- Do I have the heart of a servant? If so, how do I express this every day?
- How do other members of my family see me? Helpful, happy, encouraging, supportive? Or demanding, sour, keeping to myself, grouchy, unavailable to help, not doing my share?
- Do I have friends? Do I actively cultivate friendships by being active in my church, by being friendly where I work, by being involved in other community organizations, by helping others?

If you answered each of the above questions honestly, you know whether you are right with the world, whether you have the heart of a servant and whether your relationships with the others around you are OK. Maybe you made some notes in the margin as you answered some of the questions about things you should do. If so, move them now to a larger sheet that you can keep in a conspicuous place to remind yourself daily of the goals you are setting about your relationships with others.

Discovering, Controlling And Dealing With Self And Values

The third, fourth, fifth and sixth prerequisites all deal with the self. They are:

- Being in control of self
- Discovering and acting on personal values consistent with your Christian faith
- Discovering self and being that person
- Knowing and using your spiritual gifts

In Chapter Eleven we dealt with the topic of self-discipline. Self-discipline is the process of ensuring that our thoughts and behavior are in keeping with our goals and priorities and that we act to correct our thoughts and behavior when they are out of line with those goals and priorities. Of course, if there are no goals or priorities, self-discipline is impossible.

Being in control of self means that you have set goals and priorities and that you are able to discipline yourself to direct your energies and other resources toward those goals and priorities. It sounds easy enough, but it is very difficult to carry out. However, it is the key to most of what this book is about. This prerequisite **must** be mastered.

The setting of goals is based upon the assumption that you know what your values are (Prerequisite #4). Your goals must be consistent with those values or you will find yourself facing internal conflict. Earlier in the book we discussed ways of discovering our values. Some of our values are easily discerned; others require us to set aside time to discover. Discovery, however, should not be confused with creating. With discovery we are learning about values that we hold right now, values that guide our thoughts and behavior every day. It is just that they are in the subconscious mind and are not things that we think about every day.

We do create some values as we go through life, but they tend to be consistent with the values we have held previously. The persons who were brought up in Christian homes who steal from another person are behaving in a manner that they know is wrong, but their self-centered value is at least temporarily given more importance than the values they learned earlier in life. This conflict in values is one these persons have to deal with through behavior such as rationalization (they owe it to me or I want it more than they do).

Our Christian faith should be our most significant value. From this all other values will emanate and have consistency. Our Christian faith is Prerequisite #1. We must deal with it first.

"Discovering self and being that person" is Prerequisite #5. This deals with recognizing and acknowledging the real you. Earlier we mentioned the book by Grant Howard, *The Trauma of Transparency*.[4] Dr. Howard deals with the issues involved in being transparent to others rather than hiding behind a mask. When we are comfortable with being open with others, we also have less complicated lives to lead. We must meet the other prerequisites (1-4 above) in order to have this level of comfortableness with others. This is where the joy of our Christian faith becomes apparent to others.

The sixth prerequisite is "Knowing and using your spiritual gifts." In Chapter Four we discussed how to discover your spiritual gifts and how to use them. Once you have achieved the prerequisites (1-5), you are now at a place in life where you have few barriers (assuming good physical and mental health) that keep you from exercising your spiritual gifts. This step will cause you to have a noticeable effect upon others. You will become more obvious as a Christian role model for others. Your witness will be multiplied.

Setting Goals

The seventh prerequisite is "Setting goals and following them." Many of us experience difficulty in working with goals. One is that setting goals is very difficult for some people. Second, some people have considerable difficulty following their goals once they set them. Third, some have difficulty converting goals in their head to written goals. Fourth, some people mistakenly write down activities rather than goals.

In our organization, Oosting and Associates, Inc., which includes three divisions—Oosting Consulting, JKO Publishing and Bedford Falls Technologies—we emphasize getting each individual to think about how they will use the resource of time that they have during the week. Each person examines what needs to get done and what the priorities are among those goals. The difference between setting goals and describing activities is the difference between saying I will write and complete the XYZ proposal by 3 p.m. on Tuesday and saying that I will work on the XYZ proposal. In the first case there is a goal; in the second there is no goal, only the description of an activity.

Each of these four obstacles to goal writing must be overcome if you are to lead a goal-directed life. Are these obstacles a problem for you? Most of us have some problem with all of them. The first step in overcoming any obstacle is to recognize that the obstacle exists and be able to clearly define it. The second step is to determine what you will do about the obstacle (this is in itself a goal). The third is action, fortified by your self-discipline, to ensure that you will do what you tell yourself you will do.

Development Of Priorities

The eighth prerequisite is "Setting priorities within your goals and acting on your priorities." You cannot set priorities unless you have already identified your goals. You cannot act on your priorities unless you know what your priorities are. Some people confuse priorities with goals by saying "I need to determine my priorities" when what they meant to say was "I need to determine my goals." Be sure your goals are firmly in place, on paper, before you attempt to set any priorities among them. I emphasize again the need to commit goals (and priorities) to paper. Unless you are a person with only one or two goals, the whole process will be more complicated than you will be able to recall on a continuing basis. The written list serves also as a reminder of what you have decided as well as a chart that shows your progress as you check off items that you have completed.

Remember, priorities address the question: "Of all the goals I have set, what is the most urgent and important?" It also addresses timing. "What should I do next?" It might be that our #1 priority among our goals is something that we cannot begin for several months (like, "I am going back to college to complete my degree.") in which case we can, in the meantime, work on goals with a lesser priority but which can be tackled now because there is no timing restraint. Setting priorities does not necessarily mean that you work on #1 only until it is done. It does mean that everything that you can do now on #1 is done before you tackle #2.

Depending upon how you write your priorities, you might want to group some of them because they are closely related. Let's say you have decided to go back to college to complete a degree. There are many smaller steps that come before the first class. You have to decide where, what major? You must also get the application completed, make arrangements for paying the cost of the education and getting the transcripts sent from the colleges and universities you previously attended. So goal #1 might be returning to college. But you will have many other goals, such as ordering the transcripts, that you must take care of before your #1 goal can be acted upon. Keep all these straight in the setting of your goals and priorities.

Strategies For Prioritized Goals

Every goal must have a priority, and every priority must have strategies by which it will be implemented. This is the action plan. If your goal is to return to college and you have made this your #1 priority, then what is your strategy to make this happen? One strategy could be that you will call the college you attended before to find out how much you need to send and where to have your transcript sent to the college you are going to attend now. Another strategy might be to complete the application form, make out a check for the application fee and send these two items in the mail by the end of the day tomorrow.

Strategies enable you to move from what you would like to see happen to action you will take to ensure that it happens. Strategies need to be specific. What action is necessary? Who will take the action? When will it be done? As is true in the goal to return to college, it is helpful to have a written list when a goal requires many strategies. As you check them off when you complete them, you can see your progress. Remember that goals and priorities without strategies for action will not produce any change in your life.

The Ultimate Maturity

The ninth, tenth and eleventh prerequisites provide the finishing touches to reaching the ultimate maturity. Now, none of us has been perfect in the first eight prerequisites. But assuming we have done what we felt we were able to do and we are continuing to work on them, we are ready to look at these finishing touches. These prerequisites are essential elements that make the difference between being persons who live up to our potential, persons who live up to God's will for our lives, and persons who feel that life is still passing us by and that we are dissatisfied with how life is progressing.

I urge you to think seriously about these areas. Even if you have done everything you can physically and mentally do with the first eight prerequisites, you owe it to yourself and others around you to give attention to nine, ten and eleven.

The ninth prerequisite is "Learning continuously." In what ways do you learn? Here are some of the possibilities:

- Learn from observing the physical world
- Learn from observing others
- Learn from experimenting (doing something and seeing what happens)
- Learn from study (a goal to learn what you can on a given topic)
- Learn from reading (the Bible, books, magazines)
- Learn from listening (ideas, observations, perspectives of others)
- Learn from thinking, writing

We cannot avoid some learning experiences We have observed from the physical world that warm weather and rain bring flowers. We might conclude that we won't take that route to work again or possibly that it was a great route. We learn many good and other not so good things as a result of our daily experiences.

Yet the most important factor of this prerequisite about learning is: **Do I want to learn? What is my attitude about learning?** Is learning exciting or does it take too much energy? Is it fun to learn or do I know everything I care to know now and have opinions about the rest? Your attitude about learning will determine whether or not you will accomplish much about this prerequisite.

I am personally fascinated with learning. Learning is something I do every day. I seek out opportunities to learn. I tend to be the quieter one in conversations with most people because I can learn more from listening to others than I can from listening to myself. I also tend to be a person of few words by thinking through what I will say before I say it and then choosing my words carefully. We all learn at times by thinking aloud (whether or not others are present). Each of you will need to find the style that fits your personality. The important thing is to learn something today that is interesting and significant.

I have learned a great deal by listening to interesting people talk about their ideas and their observations. I find that I can learn much by asking questions of other people. Some people might confuse such a learning style with indecision. However, in all matters of life there are times to plant and times to harvest. But the harvest will not occur unless there was some planting. Learning is planting in our mind. We must engage in learning if we anticipate any kind of harvest from what is in our head.

Much of the difference between an interesting person and a dull person is whether or not the person has the attitude of desiring to learn (even more if the person wishes to couple this with a desire to change the world through an application of this learning).

What are some of the things that a learning person will do? Here are some possibilities:

- Listen attentively when others speak, ensuring understanding of what they heard.
- Take notes on what has been heard or observed.
- Read avidly, not only the Bible but also books and magazines in a variety of fields.
- Record thoughts, observations, conclusions.
- Have an action list of things to do or items to read that will fill in the gaps in learning to date.
- Observe constantly what can be learned from an experience even if it does not appear to be useful at the time.
- Encourage others to learn.

You will be able to add other possibilities as you think about what it means to be a learner. Futurists see this as more of a feature of the future than is present today. This is true for individuals and organizations. To learn more about how this applies in organizations, you might wish to consult Peter Senge, *The Fifth Discipline: The Art and Practice Of The Learning Organization*.⁵ It is interesting to look at the increase in the number of learning programs available for adults today. If you were to compare this to 1940, for example, you would find a transformation. Adults are given many opportunities to continue to learn today. Think about what opportunities might apply to you.

The tenth prerequisite is "Being of great courage — taking considered and consistent risks." What does it mean to "be of great courage"? Courage is the willingness to proceed even if there are risks and dangers that will come as a result of proceeding. It is saying, "I can handle the risks and dangers because what needs to happen is worth taking the risk." This is different from being foolish. When we act foolishly we take some of the same risks, but we do it without consideration of minimizing the risks and without full consideration of the gains to come as a result of taking the risk.

To be courageous requires focus upon one or more goals, energy and self-confidence. If you lack any of the three, you are not likely to act with courage. Your likelihood of reaching this goal is greatly enhanced if you can add knowledge and experience to these three (goals, energy and self-confidence). Knowledge and experience, as in anything we attempt to do, will help us to know more about what we are doing and the best ways of getting it done. But knowledge and experience are of little value if we do not have the courage to begin. Courage is taking that first step. Courage is continuing when adversity is present. Courage is finishing what you started out to do.

What is the source of courage? Why do some people have more of it than others? How much of it do you have?

There is no point to courage unless there is a **value** you hold on which you wish to take some action (which might include preventing some action by others). A value on which you wish to take action is a **goal**. Consequently, each goal must start with your value system. What are the values you hold on which you feel some action must occur? If there are none you can think of, you don't need courage except the courage it takes to face another dull day. If you can think of many, then you have many sources of excitement in your life. You are the kind of person who then needs courage to make these things happen.

Then, you must have **energy**. Some of us simply have more physical energy than others. The fact is, however, that most of us waste a high percentage of the energy God has given to us. Why do we waste it? It is because we lack goals upon which we are focusing. Regardless of our goals and regardless of our energy, every one of us spent twenty-four hours yesterday. Whether we did anything worthwhile depends upon how we used the energy we had. Were we focused upon the completion of some goals or did we amble through the day doing a little of this and a little of that? For most of us it is a mixed bag. We are more focused at some times than we are at others. Examine your day yesterday. On what were you focused? What did you accomplish? Was the day enjoyable? Why or why not? How did you use the energy God provided for you?

The third courage factor is self-confidence. God created us. We live in the world God created for us. God has a will for us. Wow! What a foundation for a meaningful life. How could we lack self-confidence with this beginning?

How do we gain self-confidence? We gain it by a series of successful experiences in life. We know what we have previously done. There is a good probability that we can do it again. The more times we do it and the more things we do, the more self-confident we become. But self-confidence is also based upon an assumption that each of us feels that life is worth living. As Christians we should understand. Read the Book of Job again. Why did Job persevere? How did he survive in the midst of all of these difficulties? He somehow still understood that God loved him.

Each of us needs to understand that God loves us and that He has a will for our lives. He expects our love in return, and

He expects us to pray to Him to learn more about His will for our lives. When we are wrapped up with doing what we want to do, we are not open to God's leading in our lives. Be open to how God would use you in this world. You will be a richer person for it.

Life can be a fearful set of experiences. Or life can be a wonderful set of opportunities. Most of the difference is in how we look at life. We will look at life in much the same way that we look at ourselves. Think of yourself as a temple of God and then look for those opportunities to serve and lead. You will find life to be challenging, but overall it will be fun, it will be rich and joyful.

The eleventh prerequisite is "Acting consistently with your faith and other values over a long period of time." All of what is said here about consistent behavior, of course, assumes that each person starts with a Christian faith that is consistent with the teachings in the Bible and that the rest of his or her value system is consistent with this Christian faith.

Our behavior is the real test of who we are. If we describe ourselves as avid readers but in fact only read a chapter a week out of the Bible, is what we say or our behavior the better descriptor? Our faith and other values will normally guide our behavior but there are times when all of us act in impulsive ways or are influenced by our peers to act in ways that are not consistent with our faith and other values. It is essential for every Christian who would guide (be in control of) his or her own life to be able to act consistently with his or her Christian faith **consistently** and **over a long period of time.**

Let's look at these two characteristics. What does it mean to act **consistently** with our Christian faith and other values. First, it requires that we have some idea of what our faith is, what our values are. This is dealt with in an earlier prerequisite. This is not something we do one time at age thirty-four and have it done for the rest of our life. We are constantly applying our value systems to new situations and, as a result, are refining our value systems. Most people today have integrated the importance of computers into their value systems. Few people had done that thirty years ago (when they made their first appearance into my value system). Some new features of society will enter our value systems this year as well. Remember that an entry into our value systems does not mean that the item becomes highly valuable to us. It just means that we make a value decision about the item. For many people, computers are near the bottom of things that might have value. Yet they have had to confront computers and make a decision about how important they are to them.

Second, what does it mean to act consistently **over a long period of time?** The term "consistent" implies at least some period of time. But what we mean here is over the years. A Christian who has served the church for forty years or all of his or her adult lifetime is acting consistently over a long period of time. Youth has its advantages, but youth cannot prove consistent behavior. They can (and should) begin on a consistent path, but consistent behavior is proven by behavior over the years. We can assume that a person who has acted as a devout Christian for twenty-five years in a particular way will not in year twenty-six exhibit behavior that is much different. So consistent behavior leads others to depend upon you for now and in the future. Sure, there are situations in which a person acts "out of character," sometimes badly out of character, as when a foolish action interrupts an otherwise consistent and wise lifestyle. Each of us needs to be reminded that if the one deviation in our behavior is a major one, such as a clear violation of one of the Ten Commandments, we will still not be considered sufficiently consistent to be trusted if our behavior is consistent 349 times out of 350 situations. Being consistent over a long period of time means that others will depend upon you to act in ways that are in keeping with your Christian faith and other values.

It's Up To You

The twelfth and last prerequisite for being in control of your Christian life is "Assuming responsibility—being in charge of your present and future." The ultimate maturity for us as human beings is to assume positive direction of our own present and future in ways that are consistent with (1) knowing the Holy Bible and adhering to its teachings, (2) following God's will for our lives, (3) acting on the spiritual gifts we have been given, (4) acting as a servant to God (whom we also worship) and the rest of mankind and (5) finding peace, joy and fulfillment in what we do, think and say. Read that sentence again.

This twelfth prerequisite is perhaps the most difficult one, partly because it requires that the first eleven prerequisites are already in place. In some ways it is a composite of the first eleven. It requires putting all the essential pieces together and keeping them together.

While God is always with us and we have friends throughout our lives, whether we meet the twelfth prerequisite is really up to us as individuals. God created us with the ability to make choices. We can make good choices and poor choices. Most of us make some of each. A major choice, however, that must be made in a positive manner is whether we will follow the twelve prerequisites to be in charge of making our lives count as Christians.

Being self-directed, being in concert with God, accepting responsibility for who we are, taking action to be the persons we can be—these can be sobering responsibilities. Yet they are our responsibilities whether we like them or not. The only option we have is what we will do about our responsibilities. Do we accept the responsibility fully for our lives?

God wants you to assume the leadership in your own life. God created you with the capability of doing this. It is my hope that this book has helped you in some way to make the decision to assume leadership and to find the ways to make this a reality. Here are some parting suggestions:

- Stay close to God—read the Bible and pray.
- Set goals for your life that are in keeping with God's will, your spiritual gifts and your interests.
- Set priorities among those goals.
- Determine the strategies for meeting those prioritized goals.

- Be conscious of the opportunities to be a servant leader with others.
- Assume leadership in your own life — work your way through the twelve prerequisites for directing your own life.

Endnotes

[1]R. C. Sproul, *The Hunger for Significance*. Foreword by Charles Colson (Ventura, CA: Regal Books, 1991), p. 14.

[2]Francis A. Schaeffer, *A Christian Manifesto* (Wheaton, IL: Crossway Books, 1993), pp. 17-18.

[3]Charles R. Swindoll, *Improving Your Serve: The Art Of Unselfish Living* (Dallas, TX: Word Publishing, 1981), p. 211.

[4]Grant Howard, *The Trauma of Transparency: A Biblical Approach To Interpersonal Communication*. Second Edition (Franklin, TN: JKO Publishing, 1997).

[5]Peter Senge, *The Fifth Discipline: The Art And Practice Of The Learning Organization* (New York, NY: Doubleday, 1994).

To Learn More

To learn more about how to develop your goals, set priorities and commit to strategies along with other aspects of personal development, we suggest:

1. For on-line access — contact Williamson Christian College at "www.williamsoncc.edu" for the course *Goals, Priorities and Attitudes* written by Dr. Oosting (credit or noncredit course).

2. Visit the Oosting & Associates home page at "www.oosting.com" for a list of colleges with on-site offerings of the *Goals, Priorities and Attitudes* course for credit.

3. For workshops and seminars — contact Oosting and Associates, Inc.

   - E-mail: "kwo@oosting.com"

   - U.S. mail: 200 Seaboard Lane, Franklin, Tennessee 37067

   - Telephone: 615/771-7706

   - Fax: 615/771-7810

Selected Bibliography

Anderson, Ray S. *Self Care: A Theology Of Personal Empowerment And Spiritual Healing*. Wheaton, IL: BridgePoint, 1995.

Arn, Win, and Charles Arn. "A New Paradigm for Ministry: Middle Adults." *Christian Standard* (September 22, 1996), pp. 7-8.

Bayly, Joseph. *The Last Thing We Talk About: Help And Hope For Those Who Grieve*. Elgin, IL: Chariot Family Publishers, 1992.

_____. *Out of My Mind: The Best of Joe Bayly*. Grand Rapids, MI: Zondervan Publishing House, 1993.

Bennis, Warren, and Burt Nanus. *Leaders: The Strategies For Taking Charge*. New York, NY: Harper and Row, 1985.

Blanchard, Kenneth, and Spencer Johnson. *The One Minute Manager*. New York, NY: Berkley Books, 1983.

Blaum, Paul A. "Henry Whitehair: In Memoriam." *Christian Standard* (October 29, 1995), pp. 12-13.

Buscaglia, Leo F. *Personhood: The Art of Being Fully Human.* New York, NY: Fawcett Columbine, 1982.

Carbonell, Mels. *What Makes You Tick...And What Ticks You Off!* Houston, TX: Rapha, 1994.

Cathy, S. Truett. *It's Easier To Succeed Than To Fail.* Foreword by Donald R. Keough. Nashville, TN: Thomas Nelson Publishers, 1989.

Cloud, Henry, and John Townsend. *Boundaries, When To Say Yes, When To Say No, To Take Control Of Your Life.* Grand Rapids, MI: Zondervan Publishing House, 1992.

Covey, Stephen R. *The Seven Habits Of Highly Effective People: Restoring The Character Ethic.* New York, NY: Simon and Schuster, 1989.

Crabb, Larry, and Dan Allender. *Encouragement: The Key To Caring.* Grand Rapids, MI: Zondervan Publishing House, 1984.

Curtis, Edward M., with John Brugaletta. *Transformed Thinking: Loving God With All Your Mind.* Franklin, TN: JKO Publishing, Inc., 1996.

Dahmen, Jerry. *I Love Life: In Spite Of It All!* Nashville, TN: Broadman Press, 1989.

DePree, Max. *Leadership Is An Art.* New York, NY: Dell Publishing, 1989.

Douglass, Stephen B. *Enjoying Your Walk With God: How To Live Above Your Everyday Circumstances.* San Bernardino, CA: Here's Life Publishers, 1989.

_____. *Managing Yourself: Practical Help For Christians In Personal Planning, Time Scheduling And Self-Control.*

Foreword by Bill Bright. San Bernardino, CA: Here's Life Publishers, Inc., 1985.

Douglass, Steve, and Al Janssen. *How To Achieve Your Potential And Enjoy Life!* San Bernardino, CA: Here's Life Publishers, 1987.

Engstrom, Ted W., with Robert C. Larson. *The Fine Art Of Friendship: Building And Maintaining Quality Relationships.* Nashville, TN: Thomas Nelson Publishers, 1985.

Finzel, Hans. *The Top Ten Mistakes Leaders Make.* Wheaton, IL: Victor Books, 1994.

Ford, Leighton. *Transforming Leadership: Jesus' Way of Creating Vision, Shaping Values and Empowering Change.* Downers Grove, IL: InterVarsity Press, 1991.

Fortune, Don, and Katie Fortune. *Discover Your God-Given Gifts.* Foreword by Rita Bennett. Grand Rapids, MI: Chosen Books, 1987.

Fulgram, Robert. *All I Really Need To Know I Learned In Kindergarten.* New York, NY: Ivy Books, 1993.

Gangel, Kenneth O. *Feeding And Leading: A Practical Handbook On Administration In Churches and Christian Organizations.* Wheaton, IL: Victor Books, 1994.

_____. *Lessons In Leadership From the Bible.* Winona Lake, IN: BMH Books, 1984.

Graham, Billy. *Answers To Life's Problems: Guidance, Inspiration, And Hope For The Challenges Of Today.* Dallas, TX: Word Publishing, 1988.

_____. *Peace With God.* Dallas, TX: Word Books, 1997.

Greenfield, Guy. *Self-Affirmation: The Life-Changing Force Of A Christian Self-Image*. Grand Rapids, MI: Baker Book House, 1988.

Grenz, Stanley J. *Created For Community: Connecting Christian Belief With Christian Living*. Foreword by Leighton Ford. Wheaton, IL: BridgePoint, 1996.

Groover, R. Edwin. *The Well-Ordered Home: Alexander Campbell And The Family*. Joplin, MO: College Press Publishing Company, 1988.

Hian, Chua Wee. *The Making Of A Leader: A Guidebook For Present And Future Leaders*. Downers Grove, IL: InterVarsity Press, 1987.

Howard, J. Grant. *Balancing Life's Demands: A New Perspective On Priorities*. Sisters, OR: Multnomah Press, 1994,

_____. *The Trauma Of Transparency: A Biblical Approach To Interpersonal Communication*. Second Edition. Franklin, TN: JKO Publishing, 1997.

Hughes, R. Kent. *Disciplines Of A Godly Man*. Wheaton, IL: Crossway Books, 1991.

Hybels, Bill. *Who You Are When No One's Looking: Choosing Consistency, Resisting Compromise*. Downers Grove, IL: InterVarsity Press, 1987.

Johnston, Jon. *Christian Excellence: Alternative To Success*. Second Edition. Franklin, TN: JKO Publishing, 1996.

Ketcherside, Carl. *Pilgrimage Of Joy: An Autobiography Of Carl Ketcherside*. Joplin, MO: College Press Publishing Company, 1991.

Kragen, Ken, with Jefferson Graham. *Life Is A Contact Sport: Ten Great Career Strategies That Work.* New York: NY: William Morrow and Company, 1994.

Kushel, Gerald. *Effective Thinking For Uncommon Success.* New York, NY: Amacom, 1991.

_____. *Reaching The Peak Performance Zone: How To Motivate Yourself And Others To Excel.* New York, NY: Amacom, 1994.

Lawson, LeRoy. *Guidelines for Growing Christians.* Cincinnati, OH: Standard Publishing, 1989.

_____. *Questions For God.* Joplin, MO: College Press Publishing Co., 1992.

Littauer, Florence. *Put Power In Your Personality!: Match Your Potential With America's Leaders.* Grand Rapids, MI: Fleming H. Revell, 1995.

Lucado, Max. *When God Whispers Your Name.* Dallas, TX: Word Publishing, 1994.

McGee, Robert S. *The Search For Significance.* Second Edition. Houston, TX: Rapha, 1990.

McGrath, Alister, and Joanna McGrath. *The Dilemma Of Self-Esteem, The Cross And Christian Confidence.* Wheaton, IL: Crossway Books, 1992.

Malphurs, Aubrey. *Values-Driven Leadership: Discovering And Developing Your Core Values For Ministry.* Grand Rapids, MI: Baker Books, 1996.

Minirith, Frank, and Paul Meier. *Happiness Is A Choice: The Symptoms, Causes And Cures Of Depression.* Foreword by Paul Tournier. Second Edition. Grand Rapids, MI: Baker Books, 1994.

Minirth, Frank, Paul Meier, and Don Hawkins. *Worry-Free Living*. Nashville, TN: Thomas Nelson, 1989.

Moreland, J. P., and David M. Ciocchi, eds. *Christian Perspectives On Being Human: A Multidisciplinary Approach To Integration*. Grand Rapids, MI: Baker Books, 1993.

Morley, Patrick M. *The Man In The Mirror*. Foreword by R. C. Sproul. Nashville, TN: Thomas Nelson Publishers, 1992.

Morrisey, George L. *Creating Your Future: Personal Strategic Planning For Professionals*. San Francisco, CA: Berrett-Koehler Publishers, 1992.

Morrison, John L. *Alexander Campbell: Educating The Moral Person*. N.P., 1991.

Packer, J. I. *Knowing God*. 20th Anniversary Edition. Downers Grove, IL: InterVarsity Press, 1993.

Peters, Tom. *Thriving On Chaos: A Handbook For A Management Revolution*. New York, NY: Alfred A. Knopf, 1988.

Price, Eugenia. *Learning To Live*. Reprint Edition. New York, NY: Jove Publications, 1986.

Rogers, Gene. *Growing In Christ*. Joplin, MO: College Press Publishing Company, 1994.

Ross, Lanson. *Take Charge Of Your Life: What Change Can Do For You*. Eugene, OR: Harvest House Publishers, 1986. Available only from JKO Publishing.

Sayler, Mary Harwell. *First Days on The Job: Devotions That Work For You*. Nashville, TN: Broadman, 1994.

Schaeffer, Francis A. *A Christian Manifesto.* Revised Edition. Wheaton, IL: Crossway Books, 1993.

_____. *How Should We Then Live? The Rise And Decline Of Western Thought And Culture.* Wheaton, IL: Crossway Books, 1983.

Schroeder, David E. *Follow Me: The Master's Plan for Men.* Grand Rapids, MI: Baker Book House, 1992.

Senge, Peter. *The Fifth Discipline: The Art And Practice Of The Learning Organization.* New York, NY: Doubleday, 1994.

Shula, Don, and Ken Blanchard. *Everyone's A Coach: You Can Inspire Anyone To Be A Winner.* New York, NY: Harper Business and Grand Rapids, MI: Zondervan Publishing House, 1995.

Smedes, Lewis B. *Mere Morality: What God Expects From Ordinary People.* Grand Rapids, MI: William B. Eerdmans Publishing Company, 1986.

Smith, Ken. *It's About Time.* Foreword by Larry Burkett. Wheaton, IL: Crossway Books, 1992.

Smith, M. Blaine. *Knowing God's Will: Finding Guidance For Personal Decisions.* Foreword by Richard C. Halverson. Downer's Grove, IL: InterVarsity Press, 1991.

Sproul, R. C. *The Hunger For Significance.* Foreword by Charles Colson. Ventura, CA: Regal Books, 1991.

Stanley, Charles. *How To Handle Adversity.* Nashville, TN: Thomas Nelson Publishers, 1989.

_____. *The Source of My Strength.* Nashville, TN: Thomas Nelson Publishers, 1994.

Stinnett, Nick, and Michael O'Donnell. *Good Kids: How You And Your Kids Can Successfully Navigate The Teen Years.* New York, NY: Doubleday, 1996.

Stowell, Joseph M. *Shepherding The Church Into The 21st Century.* Wheaton, IL: Victor Books, 1994.

Swindoll, Charles R. *Improving Your Serve.* Dallas, TX: Word Publishing, 1981.

Tournier, Paul. *To Understand Each Other.* Atlanta, GA: John Knox Press, 1974.

Voges, Ken, and Ron Braund. *Understanding How Others Misunderstand You: A Unique And Proven Plan For Strengthening Personal Relationships.* Foreword by Charles Stanley. Chicago, IL: Moody Press, 1990.

Waterman, Robert H., Jr. *The Renewal Factor: How The Best Get And Keep The Competitive Edge.* New York, NY: Bantam Books, 1987.

Womack, Morris. *Learning To Live From The Parables: Timeless Stories Jesus Told About Life.* Joplin, MO: College Press Publishing Company, 1995.

Wright, H. Norman. *How To Get Along With Almost Anyone: A Complete Guide To Building Positive Relationships With Family, Friends, Co-workers.* Dallas, TX: Word Publishing, 1989.

Scripture

Index

General Index